The Giant Book of Obscure Facts

By
Jake Jacobs

Kindle Edition

* * * * *

Published by Jake Jacobs at Amazon Kindle

1.

"Scott Pilgrim's" box office was not only beat by "The Expendables" but by "Vampires Suck" and "Lil Bow Wow's Lottery Ticket" the following week.

Reference: (http://www.boxofficemojo.com/weekend/chart/?yr=2010&wknd=34&p=.htm)

2.

Everyone has a twin stranger; someone out there who looks exactly like you.

Reference: (https://aeon.co/ideas/havent-we-met-before-on-doppelgangers-and-perception)

3.

The Aborigines of Australia were the first people to set foot on the continent, somewhere between 40,000 and 60,000 years ago.

Reference: (https://people.howstuffworks.com/aborigine.htm)

4.

A Cap'N Crunch toy lead the early roots of hacking and the Apple Company.

Reference: (http://telephone-museum.org/telephone-collections/capn-crunch-bosun-whistle/)

5.

Optogenetics is a field which may not only help restore vision in blind patients, but can bring virtual reality worlds from Matrix and Ready Player One movies to life.

Reference: (https://www.the-scientist.com/?articles.view/articleNo/50980/title/Optogenetic-Therapies-Move-Closer-to-Clinical-Use/)

6.

In 1932, Winston Churchill went to a hotel in Munich two days in a row to have tea with Adolf Hitler. Hitler stood him up both times.

Reference: (https://www.theguardian.com/commentisfree/2018/jan/10/film-churchill-hitler-tea-winston-nazi)

7.

Zebras got their stripes to keep the flies away.

Reference: (https://theconversation.com/how-the-zebra-got-its-stripes-to-ward-off-flies-24998)

8.

Andorra is one of the smallest countries in Europe. It is located among the high mountains of the Pyrenees region within close proximity to Spain and France.

Reference: (https://everything-everywhere.com/travel-to-andorra/)

9.

Dillon Freasier, the boy who played H.W. in "There Will Be Blood," was not a child actor, but a kid they interviewed at a rural school in Texas. The casting director was speeding between schools when she was pulled over by Freasier's mom who was a traffic cop. She got off with a warning.

Reference: (https://en.wikipedia.org/wiki/Dillon_Freasier)

10.

Canadian James Naismith invented the game of basketball in 1891 when he was looking for ways to keep his gym class busy on a rainy day.

Reference: (http://timeforfacts.com/15-interesting-basketball-facts/)

11.

The Beanie Babies bubble in the 1990s had $5 stuffed animals being worth up to $1,500, until the bubble burst in 1999 and they became worthless.

Reference: (https://thehustle.co/the-great-beanie-baby-bubble-of-99/)

12.

"Poop" pills are capsules containing only the bacteria from a donors' feces, which are used to treat gut infections. They have no scent, taste and are as effective as traditional fecal transplants while being much cheaper.

Reference: (http://www.cbc.ca/news/canada/edmonton/capsule-for-fecal-transplant-as-good-as-colonoscopy-to-treat-c-difficile-1.4424444)

13.

A string instruments' strings used to be made of sheep intestines that were stretched and dried and created a more mellow sound.

Reference: (https://en.wikipedia.org/wiki/Violin_construction_and_mechanics)

14.

There was a design flaw in the Huygens lander's communications system. Scientists were unable to make a firmware update on the Cassini Spacecraft, so they plotted an alternative orbital trajectory that would use the Doppler Effect to correct the programming error.

Reference:(https://en.wikipedia.org/wiki/Huygens_(spacecraft)#Critical_design_flaw_partially_resolved)

15.

A male cheetah can make a female ovulate by barking at her.

Reference: (https://news.nationalgeographic.com/news/2009/01/090109-cheetah-ovulation.html)

16.

A passenger on a Southwest flight from Atlanta to Houston fell ill mid-flight. His wife called out for a doctor, and 20 doctors who were returning from a conference stood up and helped the man until the plane landed.

Reference: (https://www.nbcnews.com/news/us-news/southwest-passenger-falls-ill-20-doctors-board-offer-help-n732056)

17.

Australian Aboriginal folklore suggests that they shaped the route of the Murray River, after its course was altered by geological uplift associated with the Cadell Fault, by cutting through a dam that had formed and allowing the river to take its present course.

Reference: (https://en.wikipedia.org/wiki/Cadell_Fault)

18.

For 3 years, tornadoes passed near or through Codell, Kansas every May 20th. After the May 20th 1918 tornado, the town never fully recovered from the devastation.

Reference: (https://en.wikipedia.org/wiki/Codell,_Kansas)

19.

Jacinto Convit, the scientist who developed the vaccine to fight leprosy, was still working to find a vaccine for cancer on his 100th birthday. Jacinto, furthermore, never charged a person for the care that he gave.

Reference: (https://www.reuters.com/article/us-venezuela-people-convit/renowned-venezuelan-expert-on-leprosy-jacinto-convit-dies-idUSKBN0DS1A720140512)

20.

In Game of Thrones, there are only five episodes in the entire series thus far in which nobody dies on screen, and only two of those, "The Bear and the Maiden Fair" in Season 3 and "Blood of My Blood" in Season 6, don't feature any deaths on screen or off.

Reference: (http://uk.businessinsider.com/game-of-thrones-deaths-ranked-sadness-2017-8/#100-ramsay-bolton-1)

21.

Ernie Hudson, who played Winston Zeddmore in "Ghostbusters," auditioned for the same character in the animated series two years later, but didn't get the part because they didn't think he sounded enough like Winston from the movie.

Reference: (https://tv.avclub.com/ernie-hudson-talks-oz-and-losing-out-on-the-ghostbuster-1798231857)

22.

On the first day of Lent, the Greek city of Tyrnavos has a festival called "Clean Monday" in honor of Dionysus. They eat penis-shaped bread, drink through penis-shaped straws from penis-shaped cups, kiss ceramic penises, sit on a penis throne and sing dirty Greek songs about the penis.

Reference: (http://www.spiegel.de/international/europe/members-only-the-annual-phallus-festival-in-greece-a-553070.html)

23.

There is a place near Sandwich in Kent called Ham.

Reference: (https://en.wikipedia.org/wiki/Ham,_Kent)

24.

Many historians believe the character of Robin Hood was based on the life of William Wallace. Studies have suggested that Wallace was a bowman, was known to be a poacher, and had a girlfriend called Mirren, which is Scots for Marion.

Reference: (https://www.highlandtitles.com/2014/09/william-wallace-birth-of-a-hero/)

25.

During a routine mission in the Laptev Sea, two Russian helicopter pilots stumbled across a previously unknown island. The new island was dubbed Yaya, for the claims made by the Mi-26 crew members crying out, "It was I, it was I who found it!", "Ya" being the Russian word for "I".

Reference: (https://en.wikipedia.org/wiki/Yaya_Island)

26.

Teddy Bears are named after U.S. President Theodore Roosevelt who refused to kill a tied up black bear on a hunting trip.

Reference: (https://hugzzies.com/blog/teddy-bears-a-brief-history)

27.

The name of the metal cobalt comes from, the kobold, is a troublesome Germanic spirit that miners blamed for making cobalt ores poisonous.

Reference: (https://en.wikipedia.org/wiki/Kobold)

28.

Sewage and gutter oil in China is recycled and used to cook Chinese street food.

Reference: (https://www.youtube.com/watch?v=vp92BlLLVEI&feature=youtu.be)

29.

While conducting DNA research on two hair samples collected from the Himalayas and believed to be from a Yeti, a leading British geneticist instead discovered they were a genetic match to an ancient polar bear.

Reference: (http://www.channel4.com/info/press/news/has-a-british-scientist-finally-unlocked-the-mystery-of-the-yeti)

30.

The "Dee" in Billy Dee Williams is short for "December."

Reference: (http://mentalfloss.com/article/93906/8-suave-facts-about-billy-dee-williams)

31.

You need at least 90 days of validity left on your passport as a U.S. citizen travelling to Europe, in the Schengen zone.

Reference: (https://travel.state.gov/content/travel/en/international-travel/before-you-go/schengen.html)

32.

The coat of arms of Paris dates from the 13th century and shows a ship.

Reference: (http://ngw.nl/heraldrywiki/index.php?title=Paris)

33.

The film "100 Years" is due to be released in November 2115. Written by and starring John Malkovich, the film is kept in a high-tech, bulletproof glass safe that will open automatically on its release date, 100 years after its announcement.

Reference: (https://en.wikipedia.org/wiki/100_Years_(film))

34.

A USB drive becomes lighter as you begin to store more data on it.

Reference: (http://www.sciencefocus.com/article/gadgets/does-usb-drive-get-heavier-you-store-more-files-it)

35.

Many people in Saguenay-Lac-St-Jean speak only French; it is the region with the smallest proportion of English speakers in Quebec. They speak French with a very thick accent that might sound strange even to other people from Quebec.

Reference: (https://wikitravel.org/en/Saguenay-Lac-St-Jean)

36.

Toronto's Chinese population will double to 1.1 million and its South Asian population will triple to 2.1 million by 2031.

Reference: (http://www.scmp.com/news/world/article/1207878/chinese-numbers-vancouver-and-toronto-double-2031-study-says)

37.

Ishi is the last known member of the Northern California tribe, the Yahi, whose tribe and family were murdered by vigilantes.

Reference: (https://www.youtube.com/watch?v=eYAUYMRTeYg&feature=youtu.be)

38.

Most watches in advertisements feature the time 10.10/22:10 because the shape made by the hands resembles a smiling face and, for some brands, it conveniently frames the brand's name.

Reference: (http://blog.michelherbelin.co.uk/why-are-clocks-and-watches-always-set-to-10-10-in-advertisements/)

39.

Toffee and caramel are basically the same thing, the only differences are that caramel has milk and toffee is cooked at a higher temperature.

Reference: (https://www.chowhound.com/food-news/54692/how-is-toffee-different-from-caramel/)

40.

According to the 2017 Global Least & Most Stressful Cities Ranking Dortmund, Germany is one of the least stressful cities in the world. It also had Germany's most frequented shopping street with nearly 13,000 visitors per hour.

Reference: (https://wikitravel.org/en/Dortmund)

41.

The most commonly found pesticide in ground water and precipitation, Atrazine, causes an induction of estrogen synthesis in mammals.

Reference: (https://www.ncbi.nlm.nih.gov/pubmed/21419222)

42.

The Currency Museum in Ottawa used to contain over 100,000 currency-related artifacts from around the world until it closed and reopened as the Bank of Canada museum in 2017. Currently, most of it is in storage and is not available to visitors.

Reference: (https://en.wikipedia.org/wiki/The_Bank_of_Canada_Museum)

43.

Australian scientists accidentally invented Wi-Fi while searching for black holes.

Reference: (http://www.nationalgeographic.com.au/australia/did-you-know-australia-invented-wi-fi.aspx)

44.

Sim cards are actually mini computers with their own CPU, ROM, RAM, and EEPROM.

Reference: (https://en.wikipedia.org/wiki/Universal_integrated_circuit_card)

45.

An accident left Alexis St. Martin with a hole through his torso and into his stomach. Scientists would tie food to a string and dip it into his stomach hole to see how it digested.

Reference: (https://en.wikipedia.org/wiki/Alexis_St._Martin)

46.

The Audubon science center genetically engineered cats that glow green in an effort to save endangered species.

Reference: (https://www.theverge.com/2013/11/6/4841714/where-cats-glow-green-weird-feline-science-acres-in-new-orleans)

47.

Queen Elizabeth II is more directly descended from William the Conqueror through her matrilineage than her patrilineage.

Reference: (https://famouskin.com/famous-kin-chart.php?name=7516+queen+elizabeth+ii&kin=3709+william+the+conqueror&via=3709+william+the+conqueror)

48.

The Islamic holiday Ashura is an optional fast day. Some volunteers will walk through the streets while punishing their bodies with whips, blades, or chains in order to draw blood.

Reference: (https://www.huffingtonpost.com/entry/why-some-muslims-self-flagellate-on-this-religious-holiday_us_57fd4ae7e4b044be3015c5eb)

49.

A bird once crashed through the front windshield of an Israeli fighter plane, knocking the pilot out, but also hitting the ejection lever.

Reference: (https://www.nytimes.com/1985/09/17/science/israel-and-the-birds-vie-for-precious-air-space.html)

50.

Princess Beatrice of York, the Queen's grand-daughter, was born on August 8th, 1988, at 8:18PM.

Reference: (https://www.townandcountrymag.com/society/tradition/a19459886/princess-beatrice-facts/)

51.

Until 2017, Mackenzie Bowell remained the only Canadian Prime Minister without a full-length biography of his life and career. "The Accidental Prime Minister" was published ten years after the author died having unsuccessfully sought a publisher for her work for a decade.

Reference: (https://en.wikipedia.org/wiki/Mackenzie_Bowell)

52.

The entire population of the United States, at the outbreak of the Civil War in 1860, was only 31.4 million people. In comparison, the current population of Texas alone is 28.3 million.

Reference:(https://www.census.gov/history/www/through_the_decades/fast_facts/1860_fast_facts.html)

53.

The level of violent crime and homicides in Quebec is far lower than almost all other large cities in Canada or the USA. For twenty months, between November 1st, 2006 and July 14th, 2008, the city of Québec reported no homicide on its territory.

Reference: (https://wikitravel.org/en/Quebec_City)

54.

Potato chip packets are made noisy to make you think the chips are crunchier. There is no reason in terms of product preservation for the noisy packets.

Reference: (http://www.news.com.au/lifestyle/food/eat/this-is-the-fascinating-reason-why-chip-manufacturers-make-the-packets-so-noisy/news-story/19784978f1d28a9b325f0e31205297ef)

55.

Giorgetto Giugiaro is the man who designed the DeLorean, along with many other vehicles, several Nikon cameras and even three firearms for Beretta.

Reference: (https://en.wikipedia.org/wiki/Giorgetto_Giugiaro)

56.

In the 1988 Seoul Olympics, a boxing match was declared "No Contest" after a boxer heard the bell ending a round from a nearby second ring, stopped fighting, and was knocked down and counted out.

Reference: (http://articles.sun-sentinel.com/1988-09-26/sports/8802250318_1_chun-jin-chul-korean-ring)

57.

Germany didn't finish paying World War I reparations until 2010.

Reference: (https://en.wikipedia.org/wiki/World_War_I_reparations#Loan_payments)

58.

Juarez is part of Mexico's zona frontera, and no visa or passport is required to enter from the United States. Pedestrians are rarely stopped or asked for identification.

Reference: (https://wikitravel.org/en/Juarez)

59.

The reason why Disney's Water County, a waterpark, closed remains unknown, although there are speculations of safety issues, deadly amoeba, and 9-11 playing a part in its closure.

Reference: (https://www.themeparktourist.com/features/20150323/30074/abandoned-rise-fall-and-decay-disney-s-river-country?page=2)

60.

The Miami Dolphins had an actual dolphin mascot from 1966 to 1968. Her name was Flipper, and she was trained to jump after every field goal and touchdown scored.

Reference: (http://www.miamidolphins.com/news/article-1/Rummaging-Through-The-Attic-Game-program-featuring-Flipper/83086675-a2a3-468a-b3c7-5dfb5ac9cf58)

61.

Clara the Indian rhino became famous during her 17 years of touring Europe in the mid-18th century. Many people considered rhinos to be mythical creatures; her popularity in Paris inspired a fashion craze dubbed "à la rhinoceros".

Reference: (https://timeline.com/clara-rhinoceros-europe-history-dc8a944c2a21)

62.

Former lovers and collaborators Marina Abramović and Ulay, famed by a clip from "The Artist is Present", found they not only shared a birth date but a strange quirk. They'd both rip that date out of every pocket dairy they owned. This revelation was a consolidator early in their relationship.

Reference: (https://youtu.be/Uw0RgkiVNqA?t=288)

63.

In 2015, Forbes named entrepreneur and CEO Elizabeth Holmes the youngest self-made female billionaire in the world. Then in 2016, allegations of fraud collapsed her company's valuation, rendering her stock worthless and reducing her net worth to zero.

Reference: (https://en.wikipedia.org/wiki/Elizabeth_Holmes)

64.

The 1982 cyberpunk film Akira, based in 2019 Tokyo, accurately predicted the 2020 Olympic summer games, of which the Olympic stadium sets the scene of the film's epic climax.

Reference: (https://kotaku.com/the-2020-tokyo-olympics-were-predicted-30-years-ago-by-1276381444)

65.

Penguin feces can be seen from space.

Reference: (https://www.universetoday.com/31894/scientists-follow-the-poop-to-find-penguin-from-space/)

66.

In 2004, Microsoft patched two swastikas and a Star of David from one of its fonts in a "critical update".

Reference: (https://www.theregister.co.uk/2004/02/11/ms_tears_swastika_from_roof/)

67.

William Shatner's first TV role was as understudy to Christopher Plummer on the Canadian Howdy Doody Show from 1954 to 1959.

Reference: (https://en.wikipedia.org/wiki/William_Shatner#Acting_career)

68.

"The Hum" occurs when a small percentage of people around the world can hear a constant low pitch hum-like noise.

Reference: (https://www.nbcnews.com/science/mysterious-hum-driving-people-crazy-around-world-6c10760872)

69.

Hockey is responsible for the airplane. Wilbur Wright was hit in the face playing, lost teeth, and needed many months to recover. This caused him to abandon plans to attend Yale and instead became a partner in his brother Orville's business.

Reference: (https://www.nytimes.com/2015/05/04/books/review-the-wright-brothers-by-david-mccullough.html)

70.

A spider called Bagheera kiplingi is known for its peculiar diet, which, uniquely for a spider, is mostly herbivorous. No other known spider has such a thoroughly herbivorous diet.

Reference: (https://www.britannica.com/animal/Bagheera-kiplingi)

71.

On Metallica's 1986 tour, guitarist Kirk Hammet and bassist Cliff Burton drew cards for bunks. Burton won, drawing the ace of spades. Hammet replied, "Fine ... I'll sleep up front, it's probably better up there anyway." That night, the bus flipped and Burton was thrown from his bunk and crushed.

Reference: (https://www.loudersound.com/news/metallica-recall-their-anger-at-cliff-burton-s-death)

72.

The only way Louis Pasteur was able to study rabies was to keep a supply of infected animals in the laboratory. His assistants routinely pinned down rabid dogs and collected vials of their foamy saliva and were under orders to shoot anyone that was bitten by the animals in the head.

Reference: (https://www.bookforum.com/review/9845)

73.

The bearskin hat worn by the Queen's Guard has been worn by British soldiers since the Battle of Waterloo in 1815. They adopted it from French imperial guards, who wore them to look taller and more intimidating.

Reference: (https://youtu.be/zak0M2Wfz9U)

74.

At a WWF event in 1999, wrestler Owen Hart plummeted to his death when the harness that was supposed to slowly lower him into the ring prematurely snapped, causing him to fall 78 feet.

Reference: (https://en.wikipedia.org/wiki/Over_the_Edge_(1999))

75.

NORAD once mistook the rising Moon for a Soviet nuclear attack.

Reference: (https://en.wikipedia.org/wiki/List_of_nuclear_close_calls)

76.

In 2006, a woman farted on a plane and tried to cover up the smell by lighting matches. When passengers alerted crew that they could smell something burning, the flight made an emergency landing and the FBI were called in to conduct an investigation.

Reference: (http://www.nbcnews.com/id/16064706/ns/us_news-weird_news/t/flatulence-forces-emergency-landing/)

77.

Meghan Markle and Prince Harry are distant cousins.

Reference: (https://famouskin.com/famous-kin-chart.php?name=6238+prince+harry&kin=80923+meghan+markle&via=26034+robert+hildyard)

78.

James Cameron sold the rights to The Terminator for $1 on the condition that he could direct the film. He regrets making the decision to sell but he regains the rights back to the franchise in 2019 due to changes in copyright law.

Reference: (https://www.businessinsider.com.au/why-terminator-genisys-had-to-come-out-this-year-2015-6)

79.

"Set the Controls for the Heart of the Sun" is the only Pink Floyd song that features all of the five band members.

Reference: (https://en.wikipedia.org/wiki/Set_the_Controls_for_the_Heart_of_the_Sun)

80.

Illinois is the "False Confession Capital" of the U.S., with nearly one quarter originating in Cook County, Illinois.

Reference: (https://chicagotonight.wttw.com/2017/09/22/chicago-really-false-confession-capital)

81.

Emilio Marcos Palma, the first documented person born in Antarctica, was a part of an Argentine solution to the sovereignty dispute over territory in Antarctica.

Reference: (https://en.wikipedia.org/wiki/Emilio_Palma)

82.

In the 2010 George Clooney movie "The American," a movie based on a novel, large sections of dialog from the main character and his love interest were lifted directly from another novel.

Reference: (https://en.wikipedia.org/wiki/The_American_(2010_film))

83.

The initial research for 3D Printing was abandoned because of "lack of business perspective".

Reference: (https://en.wikipedia.org/wiki/Chuck_Hull)

84.

An imposter named Ferdinand Demara posed as a surgeon on a Canadian Warship. He performed surgeries for a year during the Korean War using what he learned from a medical handbook.

Reference: (https://gizmodo.com/a-master-imposter-who-became-a-fake-doctor-and-performe-1711489260)

85.

Joey from Nickelback's "Photograph" had a champagne bucket on his head.

Reference: (http://www.cbc.ca/radio/q/blog/the-true-story-behind-nickelback-s-smash-hit-photograph-1.4157104)

86.

Muhammed Ali negotiated the release of 15 U.S. hostages with Saddam Hussein.

Reference: (https://nypost.com/2015/11/29/the-tale-of-muhammad-alis-goodwill-trip-to-iraq-that-freed-us-hostages/)

87.

There is a country version of rap called "Hick Hop."

Reference: (https://youtu.be/DEUm_wuCkx0)

88.

Bradley Pierce, Kirsten Dunst's character's brother in "Jumanji," was also one of the original voices of Miles from Sonic the Hedgehog.

Reference: (https://en.wikipedia.org/wiki/Bradley_Pierce)

89.

The word "gymnasium" in Latin was meant as a place of learning and a place for exercise. When it was borrowed by German, it took the former meaning exclusively and when it entered English it took the latter.

Reference: (https://en.wikipedia.org/wiki/False_friend)

90.

Borda Counts is a way of electing candidates by consensus instead of majority.

Reference: (https://en.wikipedia.org/wiki/Borda_count)

91.

Captain Phasma had less than two minutes of screen time in "Star Wars: The Force Awakens."

Reference: (https://www.youtube.com/watch?v=cwwer6_FCs4&feature=youtu.be)

92.

In 2001, the Crown Prince of Nepal shot dead 9 members of his family at a dinner party, including the King and Queen. He then shot himself and died three days later.

Reference: (https://en.wikipedia.org/wiki/Nepalese_royal_massacre)

93.

Béla Kiss, the Hungarian serial killer and alleged "vampire", killed and drained the blood of 23 women and one man prior to his conscription in the Austro-Hungarian army in World War I. He escaped arrest and was allegedly sighted in New York years later working as a janitor.

Reference: (https://en.wikipedia.org/wiki/B%C3%A9la_Kiss)

94.

There is no difference between the word "toward" and "towards", it is just more common in some regions than others.

Reference: (https://www.grammarly.com/blog/toward-towards/)

95.

Comedian Rodney Dangerfield was recognized by the Smithsonian Institution, which put one of his trademark white shirts and red ties on display. When he handed the shirt to the museum's curator, Rodney joked, "I have a feeling you're going to use this to clean Lindbergh's plane."

Reference: (https://en.wikipedia.org/wiki/Rodney_Dangerfield#Career_peak)

96.

Hernando Colón, the son of Christopher Columbus, started a universal library in Seville, Spain. He really did try to collect everything, and catalogued books, manuscripts, pamphlets and tavern posters, from weighty tomes to throwaway ephemera.

Reference: (http://www.cam.ac.uk/research/features/the-man-who-tried-to-read-all-the-books-in-the-world)

97.

The Jeffrey pine has an unusual resin from which very pure n-heptane can be distilled. This led to n-heptane being used as the zero point of the octane rating scale for gasoline.

Reference: (https://en.wikipedia.org/wiki/Jeffrey_pine)

98.

The French Paradox is the low rate of French heart disease despite a diet rich in fat and alcohol.

Reference: (https://en.wikipedia.org/wiki/French_paradox)

99.

10 billion tons of stuff are moved by ship every year. That is almost 3,000 pounds, or 1360 kilograms, for every human in existence.

Reference: (https://www.nytimes.com/2017/05/04/magazine/the-magazines-money-issue.html)

100.

A Volkswagen Passat set a Guinness Record, achieving 1,526.63 miles, or 2,456.87 kilometers, on a single tank of fuel.

Reference: (https://en.wikipedia.org/wiki/BlueMotion)

101.

After watching Snow White together with C.S. Lewis, J.R.R Tolkien grew a massive hatred towards Walt Disney, calling him a "cheat" and his works as "vulgar" and "disgusting".

Reference: (https://www.atlasobscura.com/articles/tolkien-cs-lewis-disney-snow-white-narnia-hobbit-dwarves)

102.

The largest human organ is the skin.

Reference: (https://en.wikipedia.org/wiki/Largest_body_part#Humans)

103.

Thomas Hudner was a Navy pilot who earned the Medal of Honor for deliberately crash-landing his plane to help his fellow pilot who was shot down. Despite his best efforts, his wingman, Jesse Brown, died and Hudner was evacuated, having been injured himself.

Reference: (https://en.wikipedia.org/wiki/Thomas_J._Hudner_Jr.#Medal_of_Honor_action)

104.

Osama Bin Laden had the "Charlie Bit My Finger" video in his computer's audio and visual collection.

Reference: (https://en.wikipedia.org/wiki/Charlie_Bit_My_Finger#Legacy)

105.

There are actually 3 different types of stroke, ischaemic stroke, haemorrhagic stroke and TIA.

Reference: (https://www.stroke.org.uk/what-is-stroke/types-of-stroke#Different%20types%20of%20stroke)

106.

Tupac was involved in the Los Angeles Riots and even signed looted copies of his CDs on the corner of the street by the broken in record store.

Reference: (http://www.makaveli-board.net/archive/index.php/t-26819.html)

107.

The Jurassic Park Motor Pool is a global community of enthusiasts who convert their cars into Jurassic Park replica vehicles.

Reference: (http://www.jpmotorpool.com/index.html)

108.

Saddam Hussein's son owned an actual iron maiden and used it against people he didn't like.

Reference: (https://en.wikipedia.org/wiki/Uday_Hussein)

109.

A religious cult known as the "Prince Philip Movement", located on the island of Tanna in Vanuatu, has followers that worship Prince Philip and believe that he is a divine being.

Reference: (https://en.wikipedia.org/wiki/Prince_Philip_Movement)

110.

Cards Against Humanity created a knock off Pringles called Prongles.

Reference: (https://www.originalprongles.com/)

111.

Roald Dahl's first story was written for C.S Forester's propaganda in World War II. It was about his experience as a fighter ace.

Reference: (https://en.wikipedia.org/wiki/Roald_Dahl#Fighter_ace)

112.

The world's first cellular mobile phone was demonstrated by Motorola in 1973 with a handset that weighed 4.4 pounds.

Reference: (https://en.wikipedia.org/wiki/Mobile_phone#History)

113.

Due to crossmodal correspondence, most people when asked if they see prunes as fast or slow around 83% said slow. In the case of boulders being sour or sweet, around 88% responded with sour.

Reference: (https://www.ncbi.nlm.nih.gov/pmc/articles/PMC3859554/)

114.

Supermassive black holes, located at the center of most galaxies, including ours, are very inefficient at attracting celestial bodies like stars. This, among other factors, has allowed for galaxies to remain stable.

Reference: (https://astroquizzical.com/astroquizzical/if-there-is-a-black-hole-at-the-center-of-every)

115.

Whales can "choke" to death if fish get stuck in their blowholes.

Reference: (https://news.nationalgeographic.com/2015/12/151202-whales-death-animals-science-suffocation-oceans/)

116.

Wilhelm Canaris, chief of the Abwehr, German military intelligence, from 1935 to 1944, was a member of the German Resistance essentially acting as a double agent for the Allies. He was discovered and arrested by the Nazis in 1944 and executed on April 9th, 1945, weeks before the end of the war.

Reference: (http://www.jewishvirtuallibrary.org/wilhelm-canaris)

117.

The BBC's German Service during the Second World War created a fake German resistance movement to confuse the Gestapo.

Reference: (http://nymas.org/radioproppaper.htm)

118.

Nintendo had produced a physical toy version of duck hunt in 1976, a full 8 years before the original game came out.

Reference: (http://blog.beforemario.com/2012/09/nintendo-kousenjuu-duck-hunt-1976.html?m=1)

119.

Chicago, Detroit, Philadelphia, Baltimore, and Boston are the largest U.S. cities with a shrinking population, all of them having peaked in 1950.

Reference: (https://en.wikipedia.org/wiki/List_of_shrinking_cities_in_the_United_States)

120.

The Jimi Hendrix cover of "All Along the Watchtower" was released only 6 months after the original Bob Dylan version.

Reference: (https://en.wikipedia.org/wiki/All_Along_the_Watchtower)

121.

A Ugandan mother gave birth to a girl on a flight from Amsterdam to Boston, but the newborn was considered and processed as a Canadian citizen by customs as she happened to be born in Canadian airspace.

Reference: (http://news.bbc.co.uk/2/hi/americas/7807001.stm)

122.

Mackinac Island, Missouri, is culturally preserved in time and has banned motorized vehicles for over 100 years; most travel by horse-drawn carriages and bikes.

Reference: (https://en.wikipedia.org/wiki/Mackinac_Island)

123.

The Legend of Zelda was originally going to take place partially in a futuristic setting, and Link was to collect computer chips instead of fragments of the Triforce.

Reference: (https://www.polygon.com/2012/11/4/3598112/miyamoto-wanted-link-to-be-a-recognizable-character)

124.

During filming of the Three Stooges short "Brideless Groom", actress Christine McIntyre was asked by Shemp to, "Give it to me, Chris", when she was too scared to hurt him. In the short, she really did lay blows to him, including a very real punch in the nose, knocking him through a door.

Reference: (https://en.wikipedia.org/wiki/Brideless_Groom)

125.

There are series of species where species A can interbreed with species B, and species B with species C, but not species A with species C. They're called ring species.

Reference: (https://en.wikipedia.org/wiki/Ring_species?2)

126.

Ben Sliney, FAA operations manager who ordered 4,000 planes to be grounded immediately after the 9/11 attacks, was on his first day on the job.

Reference: (https://jalopnik.com/5838772/man-who-grounded-4000-planes-on-911-was-on-first-day-of-his-job)

127.

India runs a 100% solar-powered airport, which operates with the help of 46,150 solar panels.

Reference: (http://money.cnn.com/2016/03/14/technology/india-cochin-solar-powered-airport/index.html)

128.

In Switzerland, it's perfectly legal to download any movie or games you want on internet for private usage. You can even share it with your friends.

Reference: (https://www.admin.ch/opc/en/classified-compilation/19920251/index.html#a19)

129.

The Vatican City drinks more wine per capita than anywhere else in the world.

Reference: (https://www.independent.co.uk/news/world/europe/vatican-city-drinks-more-wine-per-person-than-anywhere-else-in-the-world-9151475.html)

130.

Soccer great Pelé, could not score five headers in one game, a record held by his father.

Reference: (http://www.tribuneindia.com/mobi/news/sport/pele-s-great-regret-not-breaking-father-s-record/146659.html)

131.

190,000 stars are born every minute.

Reference: (http://curious.astro.cornell.edu/about-us/83-the-universe/stars-and-star-clusters/star-formation-and-molecular-clouds/400-how-many-stars-are-born-and-die-each-day-beginner)

132.

There's a thing called Screw-in Coffin that vertically buries people by screwing the coffin into the ground.

Reference: (http://www.cultofweird.com/death/screw-in-coffin/)

133.

King Erik XIV of Sweden, who was "in a condition of incipient insanity", and his guards murdered five incarcerated Swedish nobles.

Reference: (https://en.wikipedia.org/wiki/Sture_Murders)

134.

Bees don't actually kill themselves. Every time they sting a mammal like ourselves, they can unscrew themselves without harm given enough time.

Reference: (https://youtu.be/G-C77ujnLZo)

135.

The Hyundai Kona will be known as the Kauai in Portugal because "cona" in Portuguese is slang for female genitalia.

Reference: (https://www.autoevolution.com/news/in-portugal-the-2018-hyundai-kona-will-be-known-as-the-kauai-118381.html)

136.

Ants can teach each other in a way that both the instructor and the student modify their behavior to benefit the other.

Reference: (https://io9.gizmodo.com/how-ants-teach-each-other-and-how-to-define-teaching-1462720804)

137.

On July 24th, 1915, the ship SS Eastland rolled over onto her side while tied to a dock in the Chicago River. A total of 844 passengers and crew were killed in what was the largest loss of life from a single shipwreck on the Great Lakes.

Reference: (https://en.wikipedia.org/wiki/SS_Eastland)

138.

10 Downing Street was originally yellow. It's been painted black since the 1960s to match the soot it was determined to have been covered in since the Industrial Age.

Reference: (https://www.gov.uk/government/history/10-downing-street)

139.

At least twice, CNN correspondent Sanjay Gupta has been on location reporting, but needed to step in as a neurosurgeon: once on a Marine in Iraq, the other on a little girl injured during the Haitian earthquake.

Reference: (https://en.wikipedia.org/wiki/Sanjay_Gupta)

140.

48222 is the United States only floating zip code. The JW Wescott II is a boat on the Detroit River that delivers and picks up mail to passing freighters.

Reference: (https://wtop.com/business-finance/2017/08/mail-by-pail-is-name-of-game-for-detroits-floating-zip-code/)

141.

The man who wrote the dialogue for Portal was diagnosed with Ulcerative Colitis while working on it. He tried to quit Valve, and Gabe Newell gave him extended leave and told him that his only job was to get better.

Reference: (https://en.wikipedia.org/wiki/Erik_Wolpaw)

142.

7-Eleven is the only place the IRS allows taxpayers to pay their tax liability in cash. Payments are limited to $1,000 per day, cost $3.99 per payment, and only 34 states have participating 7-Eleven locations.

Reference: (https://www.irs.gov/payments/pay-with-cash-at-a-retail-partner#where)

143.

Lenny Montana was a decorated professional wrestler before his breakout film role as Luca Brasi in "The Godfather," winning heavyweight titles in Florida and Georgia and tag team titles in the AWA.

Reference: (http://slam.canoe.com/Slam/Wrestling/Movies/2009/10/05/11308981.html)

144.

The character "Machete" was originally developed for the children's movie series "Spy Kids."

Reference: (https://en.wikipedia.org/wiki/Machete_(2010_film))

145.

Hobbit like humans may have actually existed. In 2003, Indonesian and Australian excavation teams working in Liang Bua, Flores, uncovered the fossil of an unidentified hominin creature.

Reference: (http://www.animalplanet.com/tv-shows/monster-week/monster-articles/the-legend-of-the-ebu-gogo/)

146.

A Swedish man was arrested for building a nuclear reactor in his kitchen.

Reference: (https://www-foxnews-com.cdn.ampproject.org/v/www.foxnews.com/tech/2011/08/02/swedish-man-builds-nuclear-reactor-in-his-kitchen.amp.html?amp_js_v=a1&amp_gsa=1&usqp=mq331AQECAEYAQ%3D%3D#amp_tf=Från%20%251%24s&ampshare=http%3A%2F%2Fwww.foxnews.com%2Ftech%2F2011%2F08%2F02%2Fswedish-man-builds-nuclear-reactor-in-his-kitchen.html)

147.

The record for the longest flight in history was achieved onboard a Cessna 172 flying for 64 days and 22 hours.

Reference: (https://en.wikipedia.org/wiki/Cessna_172#Operational_history)

148.

In Doctor Strange, a dancer called Jayfunk choreographed all the magic incantation movements used by the characters in the film, using finger tutting.

Reference: (https://io9.gizmodo.com/meet-the-man-behind-doctor-stranges-spellcasting-1788581070)

149.

The founder of lingerie company Victoria's Secret sold the business for just $1 million five years after founding it, and later committed suicide by jumping from the Golden Gate Bridge as the firm went on to produce billions of dollars in revenue for the new owner.

Reference: (https://en.wikipedia.org/wiki/Roy_Raymond)

150.

After three weeks of abstinence, no change was noted in the body's reaction to arousal and orgasm; testosterone levels, however, did see an increase after the three week abstinence period.

Reference: (https://link.springer.com/article/10.1007/s003450100222)

151.

In 1993, the entire city of San Francisco voted about whether a police officer was allowed to carry a ventriloquist's dummy called Brendan O'Smarty while on patrol. He was.

Reference: (https://www.nytimes.com/1993/10/30/us/dummy-is-on-ballot-he-isn-t-seeking-office.html)

152.

When the Queen dies, Prince Charles might go by King Arthur.

Reference: (http://nationalpost.com/news/canada/what-happens-to-canada-should-the-queen-die-the-behind-the-scenes-plans-for-the-death-of-queen-elizabeth-ii)

153.

The boy who played baby Superman in the 1978 Superman movie later had a role in the 2013 movie Man of Steel.

Reference: (https://en.wikipedia.org/wiki/Aaron_Smolinski)

154.

In one of the first photos taken of Queen Victoria in the 1850s, she had her eyes closed. She defaced the photo by scratching her face off the plate. In a subsequent reshoot, she wore a wide-brimmed hat and turned her head to the side.

Reference: (http://www.bbcamerica.com/anglophenia/2014/02/new-exhibit-queen-victoria-strikes-pose)

155.

J.O. Barr wrote "The Crow" after a drunk driver killed his then-girlfriend.

Reference: (http://www.dallasobserver.com/arts/hurst-resident-and-creator-of-the-crow-james-obarr-on-the-comic-that-made-him-famous-8561547)

156.

The Podostroma Cornu-Damae is a mushroom native to Asia with such a high toxicity that it can cause multiple organ failure, hair loss and the skin to peel off, giving the illusion of radiation poisoning.

Reference: (https://en.wikipedia.org/wiki/Podostroma_cornu-damae)

157.

Diana and her sons, William and Harry, have an Indian genetic lineage.

Reference: (https://www.ucl.ac.uk/mace-lab/genetic-ancestry/guff_documents/Indian_Ancestry_of_William.pdf)

158.

The SS Imperator was referred to as masculine by Kaiser Wilhelm II's special request.

Reference: (https://en.wikipedia.org/wiki/SS_Imperator)

159.

Kit Musgrave was sunk on three ships within one hour during World War I. German U-boat U9, sank all three ships with torpedo fire. Kit was eventually rescued by a Dutch trawler after falling unconscious on a piece of driftwood.

Reference: (https://en.wikipedia.org/wiki/Wenman_Wykeham-Musgrave)

160.

One over-ripe apple can spoil all the other apples around it because of a chemical called ethylene.

Reference: (https://www.huffingtonpost.com/entry/bad-apples-rotten-good-ones_us_5784f23ee4b0ed2111d783ff)

161.

Ida Craddock, a 19th century sex educator, wrote pamphlets that advised couples on the importance of foreplay, complications of having too big of a penis, and how to properly rupture the hymen. She later committed suicide after being sentenced to prison for breaking obscenity laws.

Reference: (http://www.idacraddock.com/)

162.

The songs "Stayin' Alive", "How Deep is Your Love", "If I Can't Have You", "Night Fever", and "More than A Woman" by the Bee Gees were already written even before getting involved in the film Saturday Night Fever, as told by Robin Gibb in their documentary, "This is Where I Came In".

Reference: (https://www.youtube.com/watch?v=ul2kKH1yOFU&feature=youtu.be&t=7m30s)

163.

The American Media changed the way they reported on suicides after the government released new reporting guidance to reduce the risk of further suicides.

Reference: (https://www.ncbi.nlm.nih.gov/pmc/articles/PMC3015096/#!po=20.1031)

164.

Jeff Goldblum made his Broadway debut at the age of 19 in the original production of the musical "Two Gentlemen of Verona." The show won two Tony Awards, including Best Musical, beating out both Grease and Follies.

Reference: (https://en.wikipedia.org/wiki/Jeff_Goldblum#Personal_life)

165.

A Pennsylvania town legally changed their name to "POM Wonderful Presents: The Greatest Movie Ever Sold" to promote a new movie. The town received $25,000 dollars.

Reference:(https://wikipedia.org/wiki/POM_Wonderful_Presents:_The_Greatest_Movie_Ever_S old#sponsors)

166.

The band Guns N'Roses was named after the founders Axel Rose and Tracii Guns. Guns was kicked out of the band but the name stuck.

Reference: (https://en.wikipedia.org/wiki/Tracii_Guns)

167.

Jeremy Renner, probably best known for playing Hawkeye in "The Avengers," also owns a profitable business with his brother where they flip houses. He stated, "It's been a great outlet for me creatively... I'd probably still do it if I [just] broke even."

Reference: (http://www.ora.tv/larrykingnow/2014/12/30/jeremy-renner-0_111kka7n27yi)

168.

The first transatlantic flight was not made by Charles Lindbergh, but by British aviators John Alcock and Arthur Brown, in a modified Vickers Vimy bomber.

Reference: (https://www.youtube.com/watch?v=Yk56nBcSalg&feature=share)

169.

The Church of the SubGenius is a parody religion that satirizes better-known faiths. Journalists often consider the Church to be an elaborate joke, but a few academics have defended it as an honest system of deeply held beliefs.

Reference: (https://en.wikipedia.org/wiki/Church_of_the_SubGenius)

170.

The first black orphan legally adopted by a white couple in Indiana was adopted by cult leader Jim Jones and his wife, Marceline.

Reference: (https://en.wikipedia.org/wiki/Jim_Jones#Jones'_%22Rainbow_Family%22)

171.

Garter snakes can become toxic to their own predators by eating poisonous toads or newts, and absorbing their toxins.

Reference: (https://en.wikipedia.org/wiki/Common_garter_snake#venom)

172.

The most "well endowed" species on the planet is the Bush Cricket, with its testicles making up 14% of the insects body mass.

Reference: (https://amp.theguardian.com/science/2010/nov/10/largest-testicles-species-bush-cricket)

173.

Seagulls eat the flesh of whales, when the whales surface to breathe.

Reference: (http://news.bbc.co.uk/2/hi/science/nature/8116551.stm)

174.

The late great Garry Shandling used to hold pickup basketball games at his house featuring Will Ferrell, Adam Sandler, Adam McKay and more.

Reference: (https://uproxx.com/movies/adam-mckay-interview-basketball-ac-green/)

175.

Newton's flaming laser sword is a philosophical razor which states that "what cannot be settled by experiment is not worth debating." It was supposedly named this because it not only "undoubtedly cuts out the crap, [but] also seems to cut out almost everything else as well."

Reference: (https://en.wikipedia.org/wiki/Mike_Alder#Newton's_flaming_laser_sword)

176.

Crows hold "funerals" and will avoid an area or thing that is deemed dangerous to their own species. In other words, they know what death is and know to fear it.

Reference: (http://www.bbc.com/earth/story/20150930-the-birds-that-fear-death)

177.

The rotation of an image happens with the help of mathematics of matrices. Specifically rotation matrix.

Reference: (https://stackoverflow.com/questions/695080/how-do-i-rotate-an-image)

178.

For $50,000 USD, you can harvest a dog's DNA to create a genetically identical embryo.

Reference: (http://www.cbc.ca/news/canada/toronto/woofie-cloning-dog-ontario-1.3743788)

179.

Officials in Portland, Oregon, drained 8 million gallons of water from a reservoir in 2011 because a drunk 21-year-old urinated in it.

Reference: (https://www.usatoday.com/story/news/nation/2014/04/17/water-reservoir-urination/7814581/)

180.

An Alford plea, also called a Kennedy plea in West Virginia, an Alford guilty plea and the Alford doctrine, in United States law, is a guilty plea in criminal court, whereby a defendant in a criminal case does not admit to the criminal act and asserts innocence.

Reference: (https://en.wikipedia.org/wiki/Alford_plea?2)

181.

In 2003, the New Hampshire Supreme Court ruled that a woman cheating on her husband with another woman is not adultery because it's not technically sexual intercourse.

Reference: (https://en.wikipedia.org/wiki/Blanchflower_v._Blanchflower)

182.

Penny Marshall, who played Laverne on "Laverne & Shirly," directed "Big," and was the first woman to gross over $100 million at the box office.

Reference: (https://www.wikipedia.org/wiki/Penny_Marshall)

183.

Cats were so highly regarded in Ancient Egypt that in the event of a fire, men would guard the fire to make certain no cats ran into the flame.

Reference: (https://en.wikipedia.org/wiki/Cats_in_ancient_Egypt#Cats_in_Egyptian_religion)

184.

The Hartford Courant is the U.S.'s oldest newspaper in continuous publication, starting as a weekly paper in 1764. It claims George Washington placed an ad in it to lease part of his Mount Vernon land, Thomas Jefferson sued it for libel and lost, and Mark Twain was denied from buying stocks in it.

Reference: (http://www.courant.com/about/thc-history-htmlstory.html)

185.

Euthymia is the psychological word for a neutral mood.

Reference: (https://en.wikipedia.org/wiki/Euthymia_(medicine))

186.

In 1984, a pipe-fitter for a uranium core processing plant in Ohio was discovered in a processing furnace. At the time, the plant was discovered dumping a massive amount of radioactive waste into the atmosphere. Co-workers of the deceased worker suspected he was a whistleblower and was murdered.

Reference: (https://en.wikipedia.org/wiki/Fernald_Feed_Materials_Production_Center)

187.

Ukrainian sportsman Dmitriy Khaladzhi, performed amazing feats such as carrying a fully grown horse.

Reference: (https://fitnessvolt.com/19809/dmitriy-khaladzhi-carries-horse/)

188.

Comedian Johnny Carson was an avid tennis player. When he sold his house in Malibu to tennis star John McEnroe, the escrow terms required McEnroe to give Johnny six tennis lessons.

Reference: (https://en.wikipedia.org/wiki/Johnny_Carson#Other_notes)

189.

Mid-Grade Unleaded Fuel is a mixture of premium and regular fuel.

Reference: (https://youtu.be/F0hCl1wP-vQ?t=2m30s)

190.

During the English Civil War, Guernsey sided with Parliament and Jersey sided with the Royalty. Parliament won, however Jersey held out to the end so when the Royalty returned a few decades later, New Jersey was named in the honor of the island's leadership.

Reference: (http://www.ereferencedesk.com/resources/state-name/new-jersey.html)

191.

A yearly Wood Planing Competition is held in Japan. The thinnest piece of planed wood wins.

Reference: (http://www.odditycentral.com/events/making-see-through-wood-at-japans-unique-planing-competition.html)

192.

Volcanic Lightning, or a Dirty Thunderstorm, is a weather phenomenon that is related to the production of lightning in a volcanic plume.

Reference: (https://en.wikipedia.org/wiki/Dirty_thunderstorm)

193.

By most measures, spider silk is not stronger than steel.

Reference: (https://phys.org/news/2013-06-spider-silk-nature-stronger-steel.html)

194.

The oldest surviving example of pre-World War II live British television is a 1938 recording made by placing a cine camera in front of a television screen as the images came in New York. The broadcast was only picked up in America due to a technological fluke caused by atmospheric conditions.

Reference: (https://www.youtube.com/watch?v=0kk0ytK_nqA)

195.

Leonard Nimoy suffered from alcoholism, and at one point began drinking covertly on the set of "Star Trek".

Reference: (https://www.thefix.com/content/leonard-nimoy-recovering-alcoholic-died-83)

196.

Charles Dickens' novels were hugely popular even among the illiterate poor. They would pool their money to hire a reader, and then gather together to listen to the stories.

Reference: (https://en.wikipedia.org/wiki/Charles_Dickens)

197.

The U.S. military once encouraged U.S. hemp production and made a movie called "Hemp for Victory."

Reference: (http://www.globalhemp.com/1942/01/hemp-for-victory.html)

198.

U.S. military members aren't allowed to use any hemp products.

Reference:(https://www.army.mil/article/146680/army_regs_prohibit_eating_popular_health_bar_hemp_seeds_source_of_protein_banned_by_da)

199.

Shakey's Pizza got its name from co-founder Sherwood Johnson's nickname, "Shakey." Johnson got his nickname as a result of suffering nerve damage from obtaining malaria during World War II.

Reference: (https://en.wikipedia.org/wiki/Shakey%27s_Pizza)

200.

A recent study of nearly 2,000,000 people adds more evidence that moderate amounts of alcohol appear to be heart healthy. Researchers analyzed the link between alcohol consumption and 12 different heart ailments. Non-drinkers had an increased risk for 8 of the ailments, including heart attack.

Reference: (https://www.bmj.com/content/356/bmj.j909)

201.

The monstrous 18 liter V8 Ford GAA is the biggest petrol V8 ever built. It powered the Sherman Tank.

Reference: (https://www.warhistoryonline.com/instant-articles/v8-ford-gaa.html)

202.

An authoritarian colony was founded by a German child molester and cult leader in 1960s Chile, which was involved in child sex abuse, illegal weapons sale, torture, beatings, and murder. It also harbored Nazi concentration camp doctor Josef Mengele.

Reference: (https://en.wikipedia.org/wiki/Villa_Baviera)

203.

Florence Griffith-Joyner, the current World Record holder, set in 1988, in the 100 meter, had epilepsy and had a seizure; the seizure apparently caused her to be suffocated by her bedding.

Reference: (http://articles.latimes.com/1998/oct/23/sports/sp-35391)

204.

Snails host several types of parasites that, while may not kill them, are capable of affecting or killing their predators or animals that eat the snails.

Reference: (https://www.snail-world.com/snail-facts/)

205.

It's possible for people to have 10 nipples due to the embryonic "mammary ridge", which allow the standard two to develop, plus 8 additional nipples that appear from the armpit to the groin.

Reference: (https://www.nbcnews.com/healthmain/when-it-comes-breasts-threes-crowd-1C9926693)

206.

The Batman comic books predate the naming of Batman, Turkey by 17 years.

Reference: (https://en.wikipedia.org/wiki/Batman,_Turkey)

207.

Joseph Stalin's left arm was shorter than his right arm due to a horse-drawn carriage accident he suffered at age 12.

Reference: (https://www.military-history.org/articles/stalin-facts-10-little-known-facts.htm)

208.

It is illegal to curse in public, in Virginia.

Reference: (https://law.lis.virginia.gov/vacode/title18.2/chapter8/section18.2-388/)

209.

4 episodes of the original "Star Trek" series were banned in the U.K. when they were first available for broadcast: "Miri", "Plato's Stepchildren", "The Empath", "Whom Gods Destroy", and the episode "Patterns of Force" was banned in Germany.

Reference: (https://www.metv.com/lists/5-original-star-trek-episodes-that-were-banned-overseas)

210.

A Soviet listening device dubbed ""The Thing" transmitted conversations from the USA's Soviet Ambassador for seven years, hidden in a gifted Seal of the U.S. It was a predecessor to RFID technology.

Reference: (https://en.wikipedia.org/wiki/The_Thing_(listening_device))

211.

Herostratus was an arsonist who burned one of the Seven Wonders of the Ancient World to gain notoriety. Because of him, a law was passed, prohibiting citizens of ever speaking his name.

Reference:(http://www.perseus.tufts.edu/hopper/text?doc=Perseus%3Atext%3A1999.04.0104%3Aalphabetic+letter%3DH%3Aentry+group%3D11%3Aentry%3Dherostratus-bio-2)

212.

Live cockroaches were eaten in a competition in Florida in 2012. The winner collapsed and died from asphyxia due to choking and aspiration of gastric contents. He did, however, win a python.

Reference: (https://www.cnn.com/2012/10/09/us/florida-roach-eating-death/index.html)

213.

Because of what became known as "The Bekaa Valley Turkey Shoot", the Soviets were sharing a story: A Syrian general, upon being told by his Soviet patrons that he already had the best Soviet surface-to-air missiles, replied that what he really needed were some good surface-to-aircraft missiles.

Reference:(http://www.airforcemag.com/MagazineArchive/pages/2007/april%202007/0407eightytwo.aspx?afassoauth=MTEvMjgvMjAxNSA2OjQxOjE0IEFN%7CMTAvMjgvMjAxNSAxMDo0MToxNCBBTQ==%7CMzI=%7CODk1MzMxMTk2NTNEOTc5MUVFQkNERUM2QUZGMDlERDRBQjFFMEREUMDAxMDQ5QTE5QjBGNjU=)

214.

The Queen doesn't have a passport and doesn't need one because passports are issued in her name.

Reference: (https://nypost.com/2017/07/10/why-the-queen-doesnt-need-to-own-a-passport/)

215.

Moore's Law is the observation that the number of transistors in a dense integrated circuit doubles about every two years.

Reference: (https://en.wikipedia.org/wiki/Moore%27s_law)

216.

When Pandora's Box was opened, unleashing all the evils of the world, the only thing left inside was hope.

Reference: (http://wikipedia.org/wiki/Pandora%27s_box)

217.

Susan Travers is the only woman ever to serve in the French Foreign Legion. In World War II, she led the evacuation of her unit through German gunfire, resulting in eleven bullet holes, a shock absorber destroyed and the brakes gone.

Reference: (https://en.wikipedia.org/wiki/Susan_Travers#Second_World_War)

218.

Ikizukuri is the preparing of sashimi from live seafood and is served while still alive. The most popular sea animal used is fish, but octopus, shrimp, and lobster may also be used.

Reference: (https://en.wikipedia.org/wiki/Ikizukuri)

219.

The song "That One Night" that Jan played on "The Office" episode "Dinner Party" was performed by Todd Fancey of The New Pornographers. He made two versions, one amateur sounding and later a more polished version. The show went with his amateur version.

Reference: (https://knowledgestew.com/2015/09/20-things-you-might-not-have-known.html)

220.

Natalie Wood's original name was Natalia Nikolaevna Zakharenko, but studio executives at RKO Radio Pictures changed her name to "Natalie Wood" for American audiences.

Reference: (https://en.wikipedia.org/wiki/Natalie_Wood)

221.

Mongolia's Navy is comprised of 1 tugboat and 7 sailors, making it the smallest in the world.

Reference: (https://en.wikipedia.org/wiki/Mongolian_Armed_Forces)

222.

Geraldo Rivera was traveling with the 101st Airborne Division of the U.S. Army in Iraq as a war correspondent for Fox News and ended up drawing a map in the sand during a live broadcast pinpointing his exact location and revealing the time and details of an upcoming military operation.

Reference: (http://www.cnn.com/2003/WORLD/meast/03/31/sprj.irq.geraldo/)

223.

The photo, The Soiling of Old Glory, was taken only a short distance from the site of the Boston Massacre.

Reference: (https://en.wikipedia.org/wiki/The_Soiling_of_Old_Glory)

224.

The effects of Allied bombings on Italy during World War II were less disastrous than those suffered by German cities, mainly because Italian cities had centers made of brick and stone buildings, while German cities had centers made of wooden buildings.

Reference:(https://en.wikipedia.org/wiki/Strategic_bombing_during_World_War_II#Bombing_in_Italy)

225.

Rodney Dangerfield was rejected for membership in the Motion Picture Academy in 1995 by the head of the Academy's Actors Section, Roddy McDowall. After fan protests, the Academy reconsidered, but Dangerfield then refused to accept membership.

Reference: (https://en.wikipedia.org/wiki/Rodney_Dangerfield#Career_peak)

226.

In 1993, a 12 year old Meghan Markle appeared on Nick News to highlight sexism in household product commercials.

Reference: (https://www.youtube.com/watch?v=tfaGleA4qYo)

227.

Dr. Patricia Bath restored sight to millions of people suffering from cataracts thanks to her invention of the Laserphaco Probe. Among her multiple firsts, first African American to complete a residency in ophthalmology and first African-American female doctor to receive a medical patent.

Reference: (https://www.biography.com/people/patricia-bath-21038525)

228.

Suicides nationwide increased by 10 percent after Robin Williams' death; researchers found a convincing parallel between the increase and sensationalized coverage and headlines of his death that violated CDC guidelines, focusing on the method of death.

Reference: (https://www.theverge.com/2018/2/7/16985220/robin-williams-sucide-reporting-health)

229.

On September 11th, 2001, Officer John Perry of the NYPD went to headquarters to file retirement paperwork. When he heard the explosion at the World Trade Center, he immediately responded and was later killed when one of the towers collapsed. He was the only off-duty officer killed on 9/11.

Reference: (https://www.odmp.org/officer/15820-police-officer-john-william-perry)

230.

Receipts have high levels of BPA.

Reference: (http://www.newsweek.com/youre-absorbing-bpa-your-receipts-study-shows-230178)

231.

The phrase, "I cried all the way to the bank", came from Liberace in 1956, after a newspaper crudely accused him of homosexuality and he sued, and won.

Reference:(https://en.wikipedia.org/wiki/Liberace#Lawsuits_and_allegations_of_homosexuality)

232.

Richard Stallman rejected Ubuntu Linux because of a desktop function he qualified as an obvious spyware.

Reference: (https://ponderwall.com/index.php/2017/08/07/1133/)

233.

Former Iraqi President Saddam Hussein's wife was also his cousin.

Reference: (https://en.wikipedia.org/wiki/Sajida_Talfah)

234.

The World's Biggest Liar event is an annual competition for telling lies held in Cumbria, England. Competitors have five minutes to tell the most convincing lie they can, and politicians and lawyers are banned because, "they are judged to be too skilled at telling porkies."

Reference: (https://en.wikipedia.org/wiki/World's_Biggest_Liar)

235.

The state of Alaska has 20 official languages in addition to English.

Reference: (https://en.wikipedia.org/wiki/Alaska#Languages)

236.

Since 1984, every champion in the NBA has had a player who has been a teammate of Shaquille O'Neal.

Reference: (https://youtu.be/81ccMaThuXA)

237.

Beekeeping dogs are used to find deadly disease in beehives.

Reference: (http://news.maryland.gov/mda/press-release/2015/11/10/agriculture-departments-canine-apiary-inspector-passes-certification-test/)

238.

A remote island halfway between South Africa and Antarctica was once overrun by feral cats. To save the local seabirds the largest ever island cat eradication program was launched. Over 19 years, a combination of disease and night-hunting was used. In 1991, the island was declared cat free.

Reference: (http://www.marionseals.com/cathunters)

239.

Parts of India's first rocket were carried on bicycle and bullock cart to the launch pad.

Reference: (https://www.indiatoday.in/fyi/story/india-first-rocket-launched-from-a-church-isro-vssc-nike-apache-15606-2016-06-22)

240.

The only open-air funeral pyre in the western world is in Crestone, Colorado.

Reference: (https://www.thriveglobal.com/stories/14584-the-story-of-the-only-public-open-air-funeral-pyre-in-america)

241.

The female platypus does not have nipples but rather sweats milk out of her abdominal area to feed the young.

Reference: (http://scribol.com/environment/animals-environment/6-terrifying-things-you-didnt-know-about-the-platypus/)

242.

The Queen or King never sing "God Save The Queen" or "God Save The King."

Reference: (http://royalcentral.co.uk/blogs/insight/a-complete-guide-to-god-save-the-queen-20050)

243.

The US Army's ""Intelligence Support Activity" is a unit so secret that they officially stopped existing in 1989 and every two years they rotate codenames; some known are "Centra Spike" and "Gray Fox".

Reference: (https://en.wikipedia.org/wiki/Intelligence_Support_Activity)

244.

Ancient Japanese temples and castles had thief proof "Nightingale" floors that chirped when walked on.

Reference: (https://www.youtube.com/watch?v=jJThECzA1bc)

245.

Written words in Old English had no standardized spelling, but were spelled phonetically.

Reference: (https://lrc.la.utexas.edu/eieol/engol)

246.

Clive Wearing is an acclaimed musician who has serious amnesia after contracting herpes; he can't form memories longer than 30 seconds and always thinks he's just awoken from a coma. Despite this, he can recognize his wife and can still conduct an orchestra.

Reference: (https://en.wikipedia.org/wiki/Clive_Wearing#Amnesia)

247.

Glenn Quinn, who played Mark on "Roseanne," died in 2002 of a heroin overdose.

Reference: (https://en.wikipedia.org/wiki/Glenn_Quinn)

248.

USA's 8th president, Martin Van Buren, was the first President not of British descent.

Reference: (http://www.cnn.com/2007/LIVING/wayoflife/09/28/forgotten.presidents/index.html)

249.

The first democratically elected Taiwanese President Lee Teng-hui fought for the IJA, Japanese Army, during World War II and is more proficient in Japanese than Mandarin.

Reference: (https://en.wikipedia.org/wiki/Lee_Teng-hui)

250.

In 2015, UNESCO inscribed the Forth Bridge as the sixth World Heritage site in Scotland.

Reference: (https://www.arunastravelphotography.com/2017/11/forth-bridge-scotland.html)

251.

In the U.K., sleeping with the Princess Royal, the reigning monarch's eldest daughter, before her marriage, is considered high treason and punishable by death.

Reference: (https://en.wikipedia.org/wiki/Princess_Royal)

252.

U.S Senator Benjamin Tillman was nicknamed "Pitchfork Ben", and led a paramilitary group of Red Shirts during South Carolina's violent 1876 election, and South Carolina's 1895 constitution, which disenfranchised most of the black majority and ensured white rule for more than half a century.

Reference: (https://en.wikipedia.org/wiki/Benjamin_Tillman)

253.

In 1981, 169 construction workers fell and set into quick drying cement when working overtime to complete the Manila Film Center on the orders of Imelda Marcos, First Lady of the Philippines. During the media ban, it's alleged the bodies were covered over or dismembered to make the opening.

Reference: (http://rogue.ph/enduring-nightmare-manila-film-center/)

254.

French grammarian Dominique Bouhours's last words were, "I am about to -- or I am going to -- die: either expression is correct."

Reference: (https://en.wikipedia.org/wiki/Dominique_Bouhours?2)

255.

Nicolas Flamel's house is the oldest of Paris. It was built in 1407.

Reference: (https://en.wikipedia.org/wiki/House_of_Nicolas_Flamel)

256.

There is a hotel resort in South Korea that looks like a huge yacht that is built on the top of a large cliff.

Reference: (https://en.wikipedia.org/wiki/Sun_Cruise_Resort_%26_Yacht)

257.

The name of Siem Reap, the main Cambodian city near Angkor Wat, can be literally understood to mean "Defeat of Thailand/Siam". When Siem Reap fell under Siamese control in the 18th century, it was renamed as "Nakhorn Siam".

Reference: (https://en.wikipedia.org/wiki/Siem_Reap#History)

258.

The traditional right for only FA Cup winners being allowed to use triangular corner flags in English football does not exist.

Reference: (https://en.wikipedia.org/wiki/Triangular_corner_flags_in_English_football)

259.

When asked what he was going to do next after he failed to get his party's nomination for reelection in 1856, Franklin Pierce said, "There's nothing left to do but get drunk." He later died of liver failure.

Reference: (https://seanmunger.com/2013/10/08/our-drunkest-president-the-sad-life-of-franklin-pierce/)

260.

Elvis Presley met with Richard Nixon. He wanted to get a badge from the Bureau of Narcotics and Dangerous Drugs because with it, "he [believed he] could legally enter any country... carrying any drugs he wished." After denouncing America's drug culture to the President, the King got his wish.

Reference: (https://www.smithsonianmag.com/history/when-elvis-met-nixon-69892425/)

261.

The Contranym is a word that has two contradicting definitions. For example, shelled means both having a shell and stripped of a shell.

Reference: (https://www.usingenglish.com/glossary/contranym.html)

262.

Eight former students from Bronx High School of Science have received the Nobel Prize, which is more than any other secondary school in the world.

Reference: (https://en.wikipedia.org/wiki/Bronx_High_School_of_Science)

263.

In a survey of 284 people with Down Syndrome, nearly 99% indicated that they are happy with their lives.

Reference: (https://www.ncbi.nlm.nih.gov/pmc/articles/PMC3740159/)

264.

Surimi is a common ingredient in imitation crab and was at one point made using bovine blood plasma to help form the food.

Reference: (https://en.wikipedia.org/wiki/Surimi)

265.

Puerto Rico lost 10% of its highway funding in 1984 by not raising the drinking age to 21 in defiance of the National Minimum Drinking Age Act.

Reference:(https://en.wikipedia.org/wiki/U.S._history_of_alcohol_minimum_purchase_age_by_state)

266.

The Studio Museum in Harlem offers an 11-month studio residency for three emerging artists working in any media. Each artist is granted a free studio space and a stipend.

Reference: (https://en.wikipedia.org/wiki/Studio_Museum_in_Harlem)

267.

President Theodore Roosevelt's birthplace in Manhattan was demolished in 1916 to make way for retail space, but rebuilt to become a National Historic Site after his death.

Reference:(https://en.wikipedia.org/wiki/Theodore_Roosevelt_Birthplace_National_Historic_Site)

268.

Kingston, Ontario was the capital of Canada from 1841 to 1843. The Kingston townscape retains much of the ambience of a 19th-century commercial-institutional town and has 29 National Historic Sites.

Reference: (http://www.thecanadianencyclopedia.ca/en/article/kingston/)

269.

In 2007, an intoxicated moose named Buzzwinkle went on a bender through downtown Anchorage.

Reference: (https://vinepair.com/booze-news/buzzwinkle-drinking-moose/)

270.

Comedian Rodney Dangerfield's tombstone bears the inscription, "There goes the neighborhood."

Reference: (https://en.wikipedia.org/wiki/Rodney_Dangerfield#Later_years_and_death)

271.

At the time of his death at age 46, bodybuilder Rich Piana had 20 bottles of testosterone at his home. The autopsy revealed that his heart and liver weighed over twice the average amount. Piana was aware of his organs' enlargement and knew that it was a result of his long-term steroid abuse.

Reference: (https://en.wikipedia.org/wiki/Rich_Piana#Death)

272.

98% of the marine fish found in the aquarium hobby cannot be bred on a commercial scale in captivity; they are instead stunned using cyanide poison to enable capture, a process which not only kills many of the fish caught this way, but also destroys a square yard of the world's ailing reefs.

Reference: (https://news.nationalgeographic.com/2016/03/160310-aquarium-saltwater-tropical-fish-cyanide-coral-reefs/)

273.

The Matrix Defense is a term applied to defenses in several court cases. It is centered on the argument that the defendant thought that the real word was a computer simulation like the Matrix. It has been used several times to put the defendant in mental hospitals rather than prisons.

Reference: (https://en.wikipedia.org/wiki/The_Matrix_defense)

274.

Around 335 BCE, Aristotle, in his work poetics, stated that comedy originated in phallic processions and the light treatment of the otherwise base and ugly.

Reference: (https://en.wikipedia.org/wiki/Comedy)

275.

The Chewbacca Defense is a legal tactic that confuses the jury rather than factually refuting the opponent's case. The term originated in an episode of "South Park" that satirized the closing argument of the O.J. Simpson trial, and is now widely used.

Reference: (https://en.wikipedia.org/wiki/Chewbacca_defense)

276.

The loudest undistorted sound possible on Earth is 194 decibels. Above that threshold, the sound waves become shockwaves.

Reference: (https://waitbutwhy.com/2016/03/sound.html)

277.

"Crescent Wrench" is a brand name, not the proper name of the tool. Much like Kleenex or Bandaid, they are often called crescent wrenches because of the ubiquitousness of the brand.

Reference: (https://en.wikipedia.org/wiki/Adjustable_spanner)

278.

"Scream" and "I Know What You Did Last Summer" were written by the same person, screenwriter Kevin Williamson. He also created "Dawson's Creek."

Reference: (https://en.wikipedia.org/wiki/Kevin_Williamson_(screenwriter))

279.

An uncommon tradition in Tibet involves eating the brain directly from the skull of a still-living monkey.

Reference:(https://pdfs.semanticscholar.org/a5c0/42fb9382e07232fcb962f77082370b607ec8.pdf)

280.

The "blue ribbon" in the name of Pabst Blue Ribbon does not come from it winning a first place blue ribbon in any contests. It comes from the fact that little blue ribbons were tied around the bottles between 1882 and 1916.

Reference: (https://en.wikipedia.org/wiki/Pabst_Blue_Ribbon)

281.

The first computer programmer is considered to be Ada Lovelace, a female mathematician who was the daughter of the English Romantic poet Lord Byron.

Reference: (https://en.wikipedia.org/wiki/Ada_Lovelace)

282.

There was a lightbulb cartel from 1924 to 1939 that fixed prices and forced planned obsolescence. It included many name brand manufacturers.

Reference: (https://en.wikipedia.org/wiki/Phoebus_cartel)

283.

Princess Diana suffered a heart attack at the scene of the 1997 car crash and later had her heart massaged in the hospital before she died.

Reference: (https://www.independent.co.uk/news/uk/home-news/princess-diana-death-letter-prince-charles-accident-plan-car-paris-tunnel-crash-10-months-a7918671.html)

284.

Medical error is the 3rd leading cause of death in North America.

Reference: (https://youtu.be/auocWaG2yHY?t=24s)

285.

A typical smartphone user scrolls about 5 miles a year.

Reference: (https://www.leozqin.me/how-many-miles-will-you-scroll/)

286.

A surgeon diagnosed himself with acute appendicitis while part of a Russian expedition to Antarctica in 1961. With no other options, he performed the surgery on himself over 2 hours.

Reference: (http://www.bbc.com/news/magazine-32481442)

287.

The Earth doesn't actually orbit the Sun. Rather, it orbits the solar system's center of mass, which is very close to, but not in and of itself, the Sun.

Reference:(https://www.realclearscience.com/blog/2014/08/technically_the_earth_does_not_orbit_the_sun.html)

288.

The 1918 World Series marked the first time "The Star Spangled Banner" was performed at a major league game. During the seventh-inning stretch of Game 1, the band began playing the song because the country was involved in World War I.

Reference: (https://www.mlb.com/cut4/the-1918-world-series-and-the-debut-of-the-national-anthem-in-american-sports/c-229202336)

289.

A group needs just 23 people in it to make it more likely than not that at least 2 of them share a birthday.

Reference: (https://en.wikipedia.org/wiki/Birthday_problem)

290.

There is a joke deemed to be the world's funniest. It is based on a Goon Show sketch, written by Spike Milligan in 1951.

Reference: (https://en.wikipedia.org/wiki/World%27s_funniest_joke)

291.

Highly trained F/A-18 pilots refer to each other as "bro" and "dude" over the radio.

Reference: (https://youtu.be/tf1uLwUTDA0?t=1m8s)

292.

The difference between hay and straw is that hay has seeds in it, and straw is just stems.

Reference: (https://www.gardensalive.com/product/dont-confuse-straw-with-hay-or-hay-with-straw-what-about-straw-bale-gardening)

293.

Guglielmo Marconi, inventor of the radio and wireless technology, was an active Fascist and a supporter of Italian colonialism.

Reference: (https://en.wikipedia.org/wiki/Guglielmo_Marconi#Personal_life)

294.

Actor Gary Lockwood played Lieutenant Commander Gary Mitchell in the first "Star Trek" pilot episode and astronaut Frank Poole in "2001: A Space Odyssey."

Reference: (https://en.wikipedia.org/wiki/Gary_Lockwood)

295.

To create an accurate depiction of a black hole in the movie "Interstellar," Kip Thorne, a theoretical physicist, wrote pages of theoretical equations to help the VFX team. The resulting visual effects provided Thorne with new insights, resulting in the publication of three scientific papers.

Reference: (https://en.wikipedia.org/wiki/Interstellar_(film)#Wormholes_and_black_holes)

296.

Ancient Greeks figured out the Earth was spherical.

Reference: (https://www.youtube.com/watch?v=3EspZtA7C3o)

297.

The PRT at West Virginia University is the only one like it in the USA.

Reference: (http://www.governing.com/topics/transportation-infrastructure/personal-rapid-transit-system-morgantown-west-virginia.html)

298.

Jessica Pimentel, who plays Maria Ruiz on "Orange Is The New Black" is the vocalist of two extreme metal bands.

Reference: (https://www.decibelmagazine.com/2017/11/22/invoking-la-bruja-encabronada-orange-new-blacks-jessica-pimentel-joins-brujeria/)

299.

DJ Khaled got lost at sea on his jet ski after visiting Rick Ross's house and put it all on Snapchat.

Reference: (http://www.complex.com/music/2015/12/dj-khaled-got-lost-at-sea-and-snapchatted-the-whole-experience)

300.

Sherpa Tenzing Norgay was denied a knighthood for his 1953 ascent of Mount Everest. However, his partner Edmund Hillary was knighted, along with John Hunt, who led the expedition but did not participate in the summit.

Reference: (https://en.wikipedia.org/wiki/1953_British_Mount_Everest_expedition)

301.

Not only are narwhals real, but their "horn" is actually their upper left canine tooth.

Reference: (https://en.wikipedia.org/wiki/Narwhal)

302.

While on Earth we enjoy blue skies and red sunsets, the opposite is true for Mars. On the red, planet rust colored skies will give way to blue sunsets.

Reference: (https://briankoberlein.com/2015/05/18/two-worlds-one-sun/)

303.

Crocker Land is a fictional island between Canada and the North Pole. It was supposedly sighted in 1906 by Robert Peary, and is now believed to be part of a scheme to secure funds from a California banker for his next expedition.

Reference: (https://en.wikipedia.org/wiki/Crocker_Land_Expedition)

304.

Rick James kidnapped a 24 year old girl and kept her as a sex slave in his house.

Reference: (http://articles.latimes.com/1991-08-03/local/me-188_1_singer-rick-james)

305.

Yin Yang Fish, in Chinese cuisine, is the practice of deep frying a fish from the gills down in order to keep the fish alive while it is served. It is outlawed in Germany and Australia.

Reference: (https://en.wikipedia.org/wiki/Yin_Yang_fish)

306.

Macquarie Island is an island south of New Zealand so remote that the British rejected it as a penal colony. It's the only place on Earth where rocks from the Earth's mantle are being actively exposed above sea level.

Reference: (https://en.wikipedia.org/wiki/Macquarie_Island)

307.

Movie studios use identical twins when shooting with babies because, under a certain age, there is a limit on the number of hours that can be worked. Identical babies doubles the time.

Reference: (https://screenrant.com/roles-you-never-knew-were-played-by-twins/)

308.

Gobleki Tepe is older than Mesopotamia by at least 3000 years.

Reference: (https://www.theguardian.com/science/2008/apr/23/archaeology.turkey)

309.

The town of Anatuvuk, Arkansas, literally translates to "The Place for Caribou Droppings."

Reference: (http://blogs.sierraclub.org/layoftheland/2011/05/anaktuvuk-pass-alaska-.html)

310.

Portland, Oregon, has more pinball machines than any other city in the U.S., including New York, Chicago, or Los Angeles.

Reference: (http://www.wweek.com/culture/2017/02/07/yes-portland-has-more-pinball-machines-than-new-york-and-los-angeles-2/)

311.

IKEA started serving food in its stores because the owner Ingvar Kamprad learned that many customers were leaving without buying anything due to hunger. Over 1.2 billion hot dogs and 11.6 billion Swedish meatballs have been consumed since its opening.

Reference: (http://www.flatpackconstruction.co.uk/25-facts-ikea/)

312.

Violet Hilton was a conjoined twin who suffered the gruesome fate of dying of the flu 2-4 days after her twin Daisy had already succumbed.

Reference: (https://en.wikipedia.org/wiki/Daisy_and_Violet_Hilton)

313.

When he visited Japan as a young prince in 1891, the future Nicholas II was nearly assassinated. He survived because he turned his head at the last second, and his assailant's katana left him with just a 9-centimetre scar on his forehead.

Reference: (https://en.wikipedia.org/wiki/%C5%8Ctsu_incident)

314.

Mark Twain hated Jane Austen's books and summarized his opinion of her by saying, "every time I read Pride and Prejudice I want to dig her up and beat her over the skull with her own shin bone!"

Reference: (http://mentalfloss.com/article/32099/7-people-who-hated-pride-and-prejudice)

315.

MSG, monosodium glutamate, occurs naturally in foods like tomatoes and cheese.

Reference: (https://en.wikipedia.org/wiki/Monosodium_glutamate)

316.

"Slav Squatting" is a learned behavior attributed to Russian prison culture to avoid sitting on the cold ground.

Reference: (https://en.wikipedia.org/wiki/Gopnik#Stereotypical_appearance_and_behaviour)

317.

At a shareholder meeting, a representative suggested Apple could have greater ROI by canning accessibility features. Tim Cook responded, "When we work on making our devices accessible by the blind, I don't consider the bloody ROI."

Reference: (http://www.businessinsider.com/tim-cook-versus-a-conservative-think-tank-2014-2)

318.

The African American vocal group The Ink Spots was one of the first of what would now be called boy bands.

Reference: (https://en.wikipedia.org/wiki/Boy_band)

319.

The number of hair follicles a person has is linked to their hair color. Blondes have an average of 150,000 hairs, redheads' average 90,000, black or brown hair average 110,000 to 100,000 hairs.

Reference: (https://baumanmedical.com/qa/many-hairs-human-head/)

320.

In 1907, the founders of Neiman Marcus turned down a franchise offer with Coca-Cola to pursue the creation of a retail store.

Reference: (https://en.wikipedia.org/wiki/Neiman_Marcus)

321.

Pizza Hut created a perfume that smelled like, "fresh dough with a bit of spice."

Reference: (https://www.theglobeandmail.com/report-on-business/industry-news/marketing/all-dressed-for-success-pizza-hut-perfume-smells-of-fresh-dough-with-a-bit-of-spice/article5942472/?cmpid=rss1)

322.

A company tried to create an "uber of the skies" before the Supreme Court shut them down in 2015.

Reference: (http://blog.flytenow.com/)

323.

Men can produce breast milk. During recovery from starvation, men's glands produce hormones that trigger lactation faster than the weakened liver can regulate them.

Reference: (http://discovermagazine.com/1995/feb/fathersmilk468)

324.

Bulls is a New Zealand town toted as "Dad Joke Capital" and is known for puns. It has a sister city in the U.K. called Cowes.

Reference: (http://www.weirduniverse.net/blog/comments/bulls_new_zealand)

325.

Roughly half the mass of the Asteroid Belt is contained in the 4 largest asteroids.

Reference: (https://en.wikipedia.org/wiki/Asteroid_belt)

326.

Stanley Kubrick had commissioned a score for "2001: A Space Odyssey" from acclaimed composer Alex North. However, Kubrick abandoned North's soundtrack in postproduction, which North did not learn about until he saw the premiere screening.

Reference: (https://en.wikipedia.org/wiki/2001:_A_Space_Odyssey_(soundtrack))

327.

Alien hand syndrome is where a person's limb can act entirely on its own.

Reference: (https://en.wikipedia.org/wiki/Alien_hand_syndrome)

328.

Lynyrd Skynyrd drummer, Artimus Pyle survived the 1977 plane crash that killed fellow band members. After the crash, he attempted to seek help from a nearby farm only to be shot at by the farmer who lived there.

Reference: (https://en.wikipedia.org/wiki/Artimus_Pyle#Lynyrd_Skynyrd)

329.

The Centennial Light is the world's longest-lasting light bulb, burning since 1901. It is often cited as evidence for the existence of planned obsolescence in later-produced light bulbs.

Reference: (https://en.wikipedia.org/wiki/Centennial_Light)

330.

There was Republic of Madawaska, that encompassed parts of Maine and New Brunswick and whose flag is still flown at the Town Hall in Edmundston, New Brunswick.

Reference: (https://en.wikipedia.org/wiki/Republic_of_Madawaska)

331.

"Master Idiot" Peter Scott was a burglar whose victims include Sophia Loren and the Shah of Iran. Disturbed during a heist by a woman, he shouted "Everything's all right, madam," and she went off to bed thinking he was the butler. On other occasions, he would reassuringly shout "It's only me!".

Reference: (https://en.wikipedia.org/wiki/Peter_Scott_(thief)#Burglary)

332.

More than 99% of species to have ever existed on Earth are estimated to be extinct.

Reference: (https://en.wikipedia.org/wiki/Lists_of_organisms_by_population#Number_of_species)

333.

The SLA, or Symbionese Liberation Army, kidnapped Patty Hearst and was involved in one of the largest shootouts with police in U.S. history with over 9,000 shots fired between them.

Reference: (https://en.wikipedia.org/wiki/Symbionese_Liberation_Army#Move_to_Los_Angeles_and_police_shootout)

334.

There are hidden elves in wildlife paintings, along with other hidden mythical and Star Wars references, at the Denver Natural History Museum.

Reference: (https://www.atlasobscura.com/places/hidden-elves-at-the-denver-museum-of-nature-and-science)

335.

In 2007, NASA purchased a Russian-made toilet similar to the one already aboard ISS rather than develop one internally.

Reference: (https://en.wikipedia.org/wiki/Space_toilet)

336.

Behind Lincoln's head on Mount Rushmore there's a Hall of Records with 16 porcelain plates describing the U.S.'s history. They're kept in a teak box inside a titanium vault.

Reference: (https://www.atlasobscura.com/places/hall-of-records-in-mount-rushmore)

337.

Cats spend 70% of their life time sleeping.

Reference: (http://mediabunny.com/some-cat-facts-you-probably-never-knew-until-today/2018)

338.

Antonio Brown was fined $36,463 for twerking before the NFL changed the celebration rules. His response at the time was "Nothing to a boss."

Reference: (https://ftw.usatoday.com/2016/10/antonio-brown-twerking-fine-chiefs)

339.

Arby's purchased Buffalo Wild Wings for about $2.4 billion plus debt on February 5th, 2018, with Arby's Group renamed to Inspire Brands. Inspire Brands is a holding parent company to Arby's, Buffalo Wild Wings, and R Taco with each keeping their brands, name, logos, and operating autonomously.

Reference: (https://en.wikipedia.org/wiki/Buffalo_Wild_Wings)

340.

Japan has a popular TV show called "My First Errand" where little kids are sent to do minor tasks for the family on their own while a camera crew secretly follows them.

Reference: (https://www.citylab.com/transportation/2015/09/why-are-little-kids-in-japan-so-independent/407590/)

341.

Every dog has a "nose print", which is like a human's fingerprint that is completely unique to that dog.

Reference: (https://sitstaygoco.com/blogs/blog/dog-nose-like-fingerprint)

342.

In the 18th century, people wore fake moles, or "beauty patches", made of velvet, silk, or mouse skin as a fashion statement.

Reference: (https://www.stuffmomnevertoldyou.com/blogs/beauty-patches.htm)

343.

People outside of Japan know about Sake but Shochu is the more consumed alcoholic beverage in Japan.

Reference: (https://boutiquejapan.com/shochu/)

344.

Glenn Howerton was born in Japan, and both his father and grandfather are decorated fighter pilots.

Reference: (https://youtu.be/VWifQhqD7qM?t=24m35s)

345.

There is no requirement that the Speaker of the House is a congressman.

Reference:(https://en.wikipedia.org/wiki/Speaker_of_the_United_States_House_of_Representati ves)

346.

Albert Battel and Max Liedtke were German officers who threatened to shoot a group of SS attempting to execute Jews in Poland. They successfully rescued 100 Jews, and are among the few Wehrmacht members to be recognized as Righteous Among the Nations.

Reference: (https://en.wikipedia.org/wiki/Albert_Battel)

347.

The "Garbage People" of Cairo recycle 80% of all trash they collect compared to an average Western garbage company's 20%.

Reference: (https://en.wikipedia.org/wiki/Zabbaleen)

348.

Jonathan Frakes once played a character on an episode of "The Dukes of Hazzard."

Reference: (http://dukesofhazzard.wikia.com/wiki/Jamie_Lee_Hogg)

349.

Daniel Craig is actually distantly related to the James Bond after whom the character was named.

Reference: (https://blogs.ancestry.com/cm/born-to-be-bond-daniel-craig-and-james-bond-related/)

350.

Long service leave, employee entitlement to an additional vacation on full pay after an extended period of service with an employer, only exists in Australia and New Zealand.

Reference: (https://en.wikipedia.org/wiki/Long_service_leave)

351.

A Landrace is a pure cannabis strain cultivated in its natural environment which has never been crossbred with another variety. The strains are not hybrids, meaning they are either 100% indica or sativa, and are usually named after their region of origin like Afghan Kush or Panama Red.

Reference: (https://www.findclearchoice.com/landrace-strains/)

352.

The taunting Frenchman in "Monty Python and the Holy Grail" was historically accurate. John Cleese had the idea after reading in a history book about mediaeval soldiers whose sole purpose were to launch insults against enemy soldiers prior to battle.

Reference: (http://mentalfloss.com/article/65207/15-facts-about-monty-python-and-holy-grail)

353.

Both Mark Hamill and Billy West were in the running to voice Zim, from "Invader Zim," with Billy West actually voicing him in the unaired pilot episode.

Reference: (https://en.wikipedia.org/wiki/The_Nightmare_Begins)

354.

A hockey rink is nearly as wide as a basketball court is long.

Reference: (https://www.wired.com/2014/12/epic-fullcourt-optical-illusions/)

355.

The reason why cleaning your ears with Q-tips might make you cough is because it's an accidental triggering of a portion of the vegus nerve. In 2.3% of people, cleaning just one ear stimulates the "Arnold's nerve" and causes a coughing reflex. In .6% of people, cleaning either ear can cause this.

Reference: (https://www.thenakedscientists.com/articles/questions/why-do-i-want-cough-when-cleaning-my-ears)

356.

Tom Hanks never actually played the ping pong in Forrest Gump; the ball was added using CGI. Hanks and his competitor was just swatting air, timing their action to clicks.

Reference: (https://news.avclub.com/tom-hanks-had-some-cgi-help-for-his-forrest-gump-ping-p-1798246560)

357.

There are more Tajik people in Afghanistan than Tajikistan, and more Afghans in Pakistan than Afghanistan.

Reference: (https://en.wikipedia.org/wiki/Tajiks)

358.

In "Game of Thrones," the Meereenese rider challenging Daenerys was actually saying a Low Valyrian translation of the Frenchman's insults from "Monty Python and the Holy Grail".

Reference: (http://www.makinggameofthrones.com/production-diary/2014/5/8/interview-with-linguist-david-peterson)

359.

Aztec two-step and Montezuma's revenge are synonyms for diarrhea.

Reference: (http://www.thesaurus.com/browse/montezumas%20revenge)

360.

Charlie Kaufman did uncredited rewrites on "Kung Fu Panda 2."

Reference: (https://www.vanityfair.com/hollywood/2011/05/which-kung-fu-panda-2-jokes-did-charlie-kaufman-write)

361.

Mary-Kate and Ashley Olsen are fraternal twins, not identical twins.

Reference: (https://www.aol.com/article/2014/11/10/photo-of-mary-kate-olsen-sparks-plastic-surgery-rumors/20991375/)

362.

Gunter's Chain is a measurement device invented in 1620 which reconciled the Imperial and Decimal systems. The 66 foot long chain is also the basis for the modern length of a cricket pitch.

Reference: (https://en.wikipedia.org/wiki/Gunter%27s_chain)

363.

Some U.S. Navy aircraft could fly with their wings folded.

Reference: (https://theaviationist.com/2014/02/19/us-navy-fighters-folded-wings/)

364.

Koi ponds were originally used for a food source and not decoration.

Reference: (https://koi-care.com/history-of-koi-ponds/)

365.

There is a lake in India 16,000 feet above sea level that is full of skeletons from around 850 AD. The conclusion is that they were travelers that died from a severe hailstorm.

Reference: (https://www.atlasobscura.com/places/the-skeleton-lake-of-roopkund-india)

366.

The entire continent of Africa boycotted the FIFA World Cup in 1966.

Reference: (http://www.bbc.co.uk/news/world-africa-36763036)

367.

On March 11th, 2011, a magnitude 9.1 earthquake shook Japan and caused a deadly tsunami. As of March 1st, 2018, the death toll stands at 15,895 across 12 prefectures. Sixty-two victims remain unidentified, and 2,539 people remain unaccounted for. Tens of thousands still remain in temporary housing.

Reference: (https://www.thenational.ae/world/asia/seven-years-on-how-far-has-japan-come-after-its-earthquake-and-tsunami-1.711944)

368.

The Hongwu Emperor of China wrote a hundred word Eulogy praising Islam.

Reference: (https://otpok.com/2016/01/27/chinese-emporers-100-word-eulogy-for-the-prophet-%EF%B7%BA/)

369.

PGA golfer Steve Stricker won Comeback Player of the Year two years in a row.

Reference: (http://en.espn.co.uk/blogs/sport/story/373655.html)

370.

While developing "Star Trek", Spock was originally going to be from Mars, however, due to a concern that a Martian landing might take place before the end of the series, his home planet was changed.

Reference: (https://en.wikipedia.org/wiki/Spock)

371.

Russian author Leo Tolstoy's last words were, "But the peasants … how do the peasants die?" Seven years after his death, the Russian Revolution began.

Reference: (https://www.theguardian.com/books/gallery/2010/aug/03/authors-last-words-death)

372.

Winston Churchill, Bruce Campbell, and Wayne Gretzky are Kentucky Colonels.

Reference: (https://www.kycolonels.org/who-we-are/famous-colonels/)

373.

More collect phone calls are made on Father's Day than on any other day of the year.

Reference: (https://www.snopes.com/fact-check/we-love-you-mdash-call-collect/)

374.

A Boeing 747's wingspan is longer than the Wright brother's first flight.

Reference: (https://en.wikipedia.org/wiki/Wright_Flyer#Flight_trials_at_Kitty_Hawk)

375.

Theatre people consider Shakespeare's tragedy "Macbeth" to be cursed, and its name and quotations are forbidden backstage.

Reference: (https://en.wikipedia.org/wiki/Macbeth)

376.

Although Maryland has over 100 lakes, all of them are artificial.

Reference: (https://msa.maryland.gov/msa/mdmanual/01glance/html/lakes.html)

377.

10 bison were brought from Canada to Switzerland in the early 1990s to serve as livestock.

Reference: (https://www.swissinfo.ch/eng/wild-bison-breeding-catches-on-in-switzerland/31753634)

378.

The American Memorial Chapel in St Paul's Cathedral in London is dedicated to the American soldiers that died in World War II. It contains a Roll of Honor naming all 28,000 Americans stationed in the U.K. who gave their lives. Wood carvings celebrate American nature and achievements in space.

Reference: (https://www.stpauls.co.uk/history-collections/history/history-highlights/american-memorial-chapel-1958)

379.

Marvin Hamlisch is credited as a songwriter on Drake's "Nice for What."

Reference: (https://en.wikipedia.org/wiki/Nice_for_What)

380.

The lyrics to Bob Marley's song "War" are actually quoted from a speech given by Emperor Haile Selassie I to the U.N. in 1963.

Reference: (https://www.youtube.com/watch?v=llUTt0EmGiw&feature=youtu.be&t=9m15s)

381.

The signature line of a check is not really a line but micro printed series of words that say "signature" over and over.

Reference: (https://brokensecrets.com/2011/05/04/the-signature-line-on-checks-is-not-a-line-at-all/amp/)

382.

The 1989 Mitsubishi Minica Dangan ZZ was the first production car with five valves per cylinder.

Reference: (https://en.wikipedia.org/wiki/Mitsubishi_Minica#Sixth_generation)

383.

It has snowed on three occasions in the Sahara Desert in the last 40 years: in 1979, 2016, and in January 2018. In all these cases, the snow melted quickly, and the desert reverted to its sandy landscape.

Reference: (https://www.geolounge.com/often-snow-sahara-desert/)

384.

In 2005, 1,500 sheep jumped off of a 15 meter cliff in Turkey at once. Only 400 died; the rest were cushioned.

Reference: (http://news.bbc.co.uk/2/hi/world/europe/4665511.stm)

385.

Pluto is technically a binary system. Its moon, Charon, is massive enough in relation to Pluto that the point around which they orbit is somewhere in between the two.

Reference: (https://en.wikipedia.org/wiki/Double_planet)

386.

The term "insanity" is not a medical term, but a legal one.

Reference: (https://en.wikipedia.org/wiki/Insanity#In_medicine)

387.

In 1827, Merck was the first company to mass produce morphine.

Reference: (https://www.woodlibrarymuseum.org/museum/item/988/morphine)

388.

Winona Ryder was so named because she was born in Winona, Minnesota.

Reference: (https://en.wikipedia.org/wiki/Winona_Ryder)

389.

J.P. Morgan died with an estimated fortune of "only" $80 million, which is approximately $1.5 billion in 2015 dollars, upon hearing this John D. Rockefeller remarked, "and to think, he wasn't even a rich man".

Reference: (https://en.wikipedia.org/wiki/J._P._Morgan)

390.

The skunk displays warning signs before it can spray. They include the stomping of the feet, the raising of the tail and running towards the threat, stopping, squealing and hissing. Some types of skunks will do handstands before they spray to warn its predators.

Reference: (http://www.skunkpestcontrol.com/spraywarn.html)

391.

Stalin used a secret laboratory to analyze Mao's excrement, in order to construct a psychological profile.

Reference: (http://www.bbc.co.uk/news/world-asia-35427926)

392.

Until 1945, the U.S. had an official Office of Censorship.

Reference: (https://en.wikipedia.org/wiki/Office_of_Censorship)

393.

After he "killed" Sherlock in "The Final Problem", readers got upset and relentlessly pressured Conan Doyle to resurrect the character. In 1901, Doyle released "The Hound of the Baskervilles" in a bid to pacify, and finally in 1903, he resurrected Holmes in "The Adventure of the Empty House."

Reference: (http://www.bbc.com/culture/story/20160106-how-sherlock-holmes-changed-the-world)

394.

Taurine, a substance commonly found in energy drinks, is essential for cats. If cats don't get enough taurine, they are susceptible to blindness, heart disease, and significantly decreased reproductive performance.

Reference: (https://www.iams.com/pet-health/cat-special-concerns/the-importance-of-taurine-in-cat-food)

395.

After a grenade exploded in Lachhiman Gurung's right hand, Gurung was left bleeding, partially blinded and one armed. Then he grabbed his rifle, chambered a round, and shouted, "Now come and fight a Gurkha!" He killed 31 Japanese soldiers in 4 hours that night.

Reference: (http://www.badassoftheweek.com/gurung.html)

396.

After losing both legs and an arm during a battle, French naval officer Aristide Aubert Du Petit Thouars kept on commanding his ship from a bucket of wheat.

Reference: (https://en.wikipedia.org/wiki/Aristide_Aubert_Du_Petit_Thouars)

397.

The total of all airline miles is estimated to be worth around $ 700 billion.

Reference: (https://www.rollingstone.com/culture/features/ben-schlappig-airlines-fly-free-20150720)

398.

"Get Out" was shot in only 23 days due to budget constraints.

Reference: (https://www.if.com.au/cinematographer-toby-oliver-shooting-get/)

399.

A New Zealand spy once lost his briefcase. It was found to contain his business card, 5 pies, a diary, and a copy of Penthouse, a pornographic magazine.

Reference: (https://www.nzherald.co.nz/nz/news/article.cfm?c_id=1&objectid=11451304)

400.

Giraffes are becoming endangered, with a 40% population decline in the last 30 years. There are fewer giraffes in Africa than elephants.

Reference: (http://time.com/4750296/giraffes-endangered-list/)

401.

The co-founder of Atari also founded Chuck E. Cheese.

Reference: (https://en.wikipedia.org/wiki/Chuck_E._Cheese%27s)

402.

The distinctive rag-time piano portion of Bachman-Turner Overdrive's rock classic "Takin' Care of Business" was played by a pizza-delivery guy who happened to have the fortune of delivering pizza to their studio early in the morning.

Reference: (https://www.youtube.com/watch?v=Tb4PE70Da04)

403.

The famous exploding head scene from the movie "Scanners" was achieved by blasting the back of the head with a shotgun.

Reference: (https://news.avclub.com/here-s-how-special-effects-artists-created-the-explodin-1798270340)

404.

There are video games made just for one specific player and can cost up to $67,000.

Reference: (https://en.wikipedia.org/wiki/Personalized_video_game)

405.

Creed Bratton from "The Office" is actually a fictionalized version of the actor who portrays him, Creed Bratton.

Reference: (https://en.wikipedia.org/wiki/Creed_Bratton)

406.

Coleslaw gets its name from the Dutch "koolsla" meaning "cabbage salad".

Reference: (https://en.wikipedia.org/wiki/Coleslaw)

407.

There are more than 87,000 glassing attacks in the U.K. every year.

Reference: (https://en.wikipedia.org/wiki/Glassing)

408.

"The Groom(s) of the King's Close Stool" were courtiers of the English monarch that assisted him in excretion and hygiene. These courtiers were considered to be the closest confidants of the monarch and some even became early prime ministers.

Reference: (https://www.historyextra.com/period/who-was-the-last-groom-of-the-stool/)

409.

When Tom Green won a Golden Raspberry Award for "Freddy Got Fingered", he showed up in a white Cadillac, rolled out his own red carpet, told the crowd he wanted to win the award, then pulled out and played a harmonica until security dragged him offstage.

Reference: (https://en.wikipedia.org/wiki/Tom_Green)

410.

Tim Tomeshek was eating a hotdog in the audience of a boxing match and filled in for a boxer that pulled out of the fight. Tim Tomeshek took the fight on 2 hours' notice.

Reference: (https://www.youtube.com/watch?v=Ey91V6NF-mw)

411.

After eating "palatable" chocolate, a negative mood improves, but the effect disappears after only 3 minutes. "Unpalatable" chocolate has no effect, so researchers conclude that the effect is caused by the palatability.

Reference: (https://www.ncbi.nlm.nih.gov/pubmed/17597253)

412.

Taylor Muhl is a woman with a unique birthmark where one side of her body is redder than the other half, due to a rare medical condition called tetramagetic chimerism, where she has two sets of DNA in her body. She is literally her own twin.

Reference: (http://www.businessinsider.com/taylor-muhl-birthmark-discovers-shes-her-own-twin-2018-3/?r=AU&IR=T)

413.

During the famed "Dame Busters" raid, bombers flew so low that one plane on the way to their target clipped the sea, losing its bomb in the process, recovered and flew back to base. Two other bombers later crashed due to collisions with power-lines.

Reference: (https://en.wikipedia.org/wiki/Operation_Chastise#The_attacks)

414.

The story that was the basis for "The Iron Giant" was written by Sylvia Plath's husband to entertain their children.

Reference: (https://en.wikipedia.org/wiki/The_Iron_Giant)

415.

A quadripoint is a point on the Earth that touches the border of four distinct territories. The only true one ever existed briefly between 1960 and 1961 in Africa.

Reference: (https://en.wikipedia.org/wiki/Quadripoint)

416.

In Alaska, it is illegal to be drunk in a bar.

Reference: (https://www.rd.com/funny-stuff/dumbest-laws-america/)

417.

Baseball player Stan Musial demanded his pay check be cut by $20,000 after he had a subpar year in 1959.

Reference: (https://www.usatoday.com/story/sports/mlb/2013/01/20/stan-musial-six-things-to-know-about-the-man-hall-of-famer-dead/1848737/)

418.

A family-owned coin shop in Massachusetts is the largest seller of raw gold to the U.S. government with a revenue of $6.5 billion as of 2011.

Reference: (https://www.bloomberg.com/news/articles/2011-11-03/the-family-that-sells-gold-to-the-government)

419.

Freddie Mercury, after his death, gave his assistant and chef £500,000 each and £100,000 for his driver.

Reference: (http://www.freddie.ru/e/archives/daily_mail/)

420.

Diarrhea was one of the most common causes of death in the American Civil War and soldiers had an unwritten code of honor against shooting someone who was defecating.

Reference: (https://academic.oup.com/jhmas/article-abstract/47/1/49/770426)

421.

Samoyeds actually come in 3 different colors: black, white, and biscuit.

Reference: (https://samoyedlife.com/samoyed-colour-varieties)

422.

We share as much genetic similarity with our friends as with 4th cousins, not because of shared ethnic backgrounds, but because of positive selection for complementary immune traits.

Reference: (https://www.nature.com/scitable/blog/accumulating-glitches/friends_are_genetically_similar)

423.

The term "Nickelodeon" was used for early movie theaters that cost 5¢ to enter. An "odeon" was any building used for live entertainment in ancient Greece and Rome.

Reference: (https://en.wikipedia.org/wiki/Odeon_(building))

424.

Practicing something in a lucid dream improves your real world performance.

Reference: (https://journals.humankinetics.com/doi/abs/10.1123/tsp.24.2.157)

425.

Over half of the world's lentils are grown in Canada, with about 95% that amount grown in the province of Saskatchewan alone.

Reference: (https://en.wikipedia.org/wiki/Lentil#Production)

426.

In 1894, John Jacob Astor IV, who died during the sinking of the Titanic, wrote a book about a manned mission to Jupiter in 2001.

Reference: (http://www.gutenberg.org/ebooks/1607?msg=welcome_stranger)

427.

Herbert Hoover was so fat that his doctor invented Hooverball, where "On a tennis-like court, two teams of three players throw a 6-pound medicine ball back and forth over an 8-foot net." Hoover lost 21 pounds in his term.

Reference: (https://www.futilitycloset.com/2014/09/26/hooverball/)

428.

John Travolta adapted L. Ron Hubbard's novel "Battlefield Earth" into a film directed by George Lucas' protégé. Travolta described it as, "like Star Wars, only better!", however, the film was a commercial and critical failure and grossed less than half its budget.

Reference: (https://en.wikipedia.org/wiki/Battlefield_Earth_(film))

429.

Punxsutawney Phil has about a 35% to 40% accuracy rate in predicting if winter will last 6 more weeks or not.

Reference: (https://en.wikipedia.org/wiki/Punxsutawney_Phil)

430.

The U.S. government has approved a proposal to release bio-engineered "killer" mosquitoes into the environment. They harbor a particular bacterial pathogen designed to infect and kill other mosquitoes.

Reference: (https://www.nature.com/news/us-government-approves-killer-mosquitoes-to-fight-disease-1.22959)

431.

The briefcase in "Pulp Fiction" originally contained diamonds but that was deemed too predictable so it was decided that the contents were never to be seen. This way each audience member would fill in the blank with their own contents.

Reference: (https://www.snopes.com/fact-check/whats-in-the-briefcase/)

432.

Ciabatta has only been around since 1982.

Reference: (https://en.wikipedia.org/wiki/Ciabatta)

433.

Ioannis Ikonomou, the Chief Translator for the European Commission, reportedly knows as many as 47 languages and learned 15 languages by the age of 20.

Reference: (https://en.wikipedia.org/wiki/Ioannis_Ikonomou)

434.

Newborns have greater concentrations of gold in their hair compared to older children and adults.

Reference: (https://www.ncbi.nlm.nih.gov/pubmed/6498011)

435.

Brian Eno wrote the Windows 95 startup sound on a Mac.

Reference: (https://en.wikipedia.org/wiki/Brian_Eno#The_Microsoft_Sound)

436.

The famous interlocking "NY" logo of the New York Yankees predates the baseball team. It was first designed by Tiffany and Co. as part of a Medal of Valor for John McDowell, an NYPD officer who was shot in the line of duty in 1877.

Reference: (https://www.amny.com/secrets-of-new-york/new-york-yankees-jersey-cap-and-logo-history-1.10642825)

437.

Mama Cass of "the Mama's & the Papa's" died at 32 in a flat owned by singer and songwriter Harry Nilsson. The Who's Keith Moon wanted to rent the flat from Nilsson who didn't want to rent it out because he thought it was cursed. Reluctantly, he rented it to Moon who later died in the same room as Cass at age 32.

Reference: (https://en.wikipedia.org/wiki/Keith_Moon)

438.

The Stanley of Stanley Thermos is the father of Stanley from Morgan Stanley.

Reference: (https://en.wikipedia.org/wiki/William_Stanley_Jr.#Personal_life)

439.

The domain name ".tv" is the domain representing the country of Tuvalu. In 1998, Tuvalu signed a contract for the exclusive marketing rights for the domain name, allowing it to finally raise enough money to join the United Nations.

Reference: (http://www.news.com.au/technology/the-island-nation-of-tuvalu-is-being-kept-afloat-by-its-domain-name/news-story/9af6c78e14c071013ddd7fa9ac64aa7f)

440.

The "Fovea centralis" is the tiny pit in the retina where 20/20 vision is attainable. It's a cognitive illusion that we see sharply across all of our vision.

Reference: (https://en.wikipedia.org/wiki/Fovea_centralis)

441.

During the Holocaust, the Nazis targeted people who spoke Esperanto, a language that was created in 1889 to unite the world and serve as a universal language for humanity.

Reference: (https://en.wikipedia.org/wiki/Esperanto#Later_history)

442.

A 12 year old Norwegian boy managed to survive a moose attack using tactics learned from playing World of Warcraft.

Reference: (https://www.wired.com/2007/12/boy-survives-mo/)

443.

In 1404, England passed a law prohibiting alchemists from using their knowledge to create precious metals.

Reference: (https://www.onthisday.com/date/1404/january/13)

444.

Michael Crichton, author of Jurassic Park, has a dinosaur genus named after him.

Reference: (https://en.wikipedia.org/wiki/Crichtonsaurus)

445.

Marcella LeBeau, a World War II army nurse, served in the wake of D-Day and the Battle of the Bulge. She received the French Legion of Honor, the highest French order of merit for military and civil merits. The Native American woman is 98 and still active in her community in South Dakota.

Reference: (http://rapidcityjournal.com/news/local/wwii-nurse-overcame-obstacles-helped-soldiers-heal/article_703beedd-c11f-5db4-a948-15121bf0e83e.html)

446.

The song "'Stone Cold Crazy" by Queen is considered to be the earliest example of thrash metal.

Reference: (https://en.wikipedia.org/wiki/Stone_Cold_Crazy)

447.

There was once a Scottish Court set up in an old U.S. Air Force base in Utrecht, Netherlands to prosecute Libyan citizens who were on trial for the bombing of a Pan Am flight.

Reference: (https://en.wikipedia.org/wiki/Scottish_Court_in_the_Netherlands)

448.

Mila Kunis was just 14 years old when she got the role of Jackie Burkhart in the show "That '70s Show" claiming that she was turning 18 years old.

Reference: (https://en.wikipedia.org/wiki/Mila_Kunis)

449.

During the Cold War, the communist government in Poland stated that American planes dropped thousands of potato beetles on polish crops in order to wage sabotage and diversionary actions aimed at socialist Poland.

Reference:(https://en.wikipedia.org/wiki/War_against_the_potato_beetle#People's_Republic_of_Poland)

450.

In the bubonic plague's aftermath, wages in England rose from 12% to 28% from the 1340s to the 1350s and 20% to 40% from the 1340s to the 1360s.

Reference: (https://eh.net/encyclopedia/the-economic-impact-of-the-black-death/)

451.

Montpelier is the only state capital in the United States that does not have a McDonald's.

Reference: (http://www.businessinsider.com/montpelier-doesnt-have-a-mcdonalds-2017-12)

452.

When a person drowns, their lungs don't actually fill with water, rather due to the laryngeal spasm that occurs, they suffocate, as a result of realizing they are drowning.

Reference: (https://www.youtube.com/watch?v=mx8cDDB6OQM&feature=youtu.be)

453.

It's illegal in Florida to charge more to pay by credit card, but legal to offer a discount to pay by cash.

Reference: (https://www.cardsystems.com/2017/08/10/credit-card-surcharges-prohibited/)

454.

Thomas "Tiny" Lister Jr., the antagonist in "Friday" and President Lindberg in "The Fifth Element" is blind in his right eye.

Reference: (https://en.wikipedia.org/wiki/Tom_Lister_Jr.)

455.

A man riding his bicycle down an icy road in Finland was struck by a truck and killed. A little more than two hours later, the man's twin brother was struck and killed by another truck while riding his bicycle about one mile from the first accident.

Reference: (https://www.nytimes.com/2002/03/07/world/world-briefing-europe-finland-twins-die-in-nearly-identical-accidents.html)

456.

Laser Blended Vision is a form of LASIK surgery that corrects both near and distance vision.

Reference: (https://en.wikipedia.org/wiki/Laser_blended_vision)

457.

Moray Eels have a second jaw which grabs its prey further into its mouth.

Reference: (http://sciencenotes.ucsc.edu/2014/pages/eels/eels.html)

458.

A man lived with a bullet in his head for five years after forgetting he was shot at party. When presented with the bullet, the man recalled that he had received a blow to the head around midnight at a New Year's party 5 years prior but had forgotten about it because he had been "very drunk".

Reference: (https://www.reuters.com/article/us-germany-bullet-odd/man-shot-in-head-notices-five-years-later-idUSTRE67N3XL20100824)

459.

CliffsNotes originated in Canada as Coles Notes, and there are still two different versions for each country today.

Reference: (https://www.cliffsnotes.com/discover-about)

460.

The first baseball team to play in what is now known as Wrigley Field was the Chicago Whales of the short lived Federal League.

Reference: (https://en.wikipedia.org/wiki/Chicago_Whales)

461.

El Helicoide is a pyramid shaped prison in Venezuela that is a former shopping center. In addition to being a prison, it is also the headquarters of the National Experimental University of Security.

Reference: (https://www.citylab.com/design/2017/05/how-an-icon-of-venezuelan-architecture-became-a-prison/528270/)

462.

In the late 1980s, George Lucas did a series of Japanese commercials for Panasonic in honor of A New Hope's 10th anniversary.

Reference: (http://www.slashfilm.com/japanese-star-wars-panasonic-commercials/)

463.

Bridesmaids all wear matching colors because of an old tradition that dictated they not only dress like each other but like the bride herself in order to confuse evil spirits or those who wished to harm the bride.

Reference: (https://www.rd.com/culture/history-of-bridesmaids-weddings/)

464.

Actor Rob Riggle was a Marine for 23 years, was a lieutenant colonel, and has received a combat award for his service in Kosovo, Afghanistan, and Liberia.

Reference: (https://en.wikipedia.org/wiki/Rob_Riggle#Military_career)

465.

After the 2012 Italian cruise ship disaster of the Costa Concordia capsizing off the Italian Coast, investigators learned that the cruise ship was carrying a huge shipment of mafia-owned cocaine.

Reference: (https://www.independent.co.uk/news/world/europe/costa-concordia-shipment-of-mob-drugs-was-hidden-aboard-cruise-liner-when-it-hit-rocks-off-italian-10144558.html)

466.

The Panama Canal was arguably the deadliest construction project ever, with an estimated 408 construction worker deaths per 1,000 workers, totaling in over 30,000 worker deaths during the life of the project.

Reference: (https://www.forconstructionpros.com/blogs/construction-toolbox/blog/12096401/looking-back-on-the-worlds-deadliest-construction-projects)

467.

La Rinconada, Peru, the highest town on Earth, lies at an altitude of almost 17,000 feet, or 5000 meters, nearly as high as Everest Base Camp. It has no infrastructure, and miners receive no pay except for being allowed to keep the gold they find on the last day of each month.

Reference: (http://www.businessinsider.com/living-in-la-rinconada-the-highest-habitable-place-on-earth-2016-12#the-settlement-has-been-built-at-an-astonishing-height-of-16700-feet-and-lies-in-the-shadow-of-bella-durmiente-or-sleeping-beauty-an-enormous-glacier-that-lurks-over-the-town-2)

468.

After crashing during the 1984 Dallas Grand Prix, Ayrton Senna's excuse was that the, "wall must have moved". Nobody believed him, until he insisted it was checked. The wall had moved less than half an inch nearer the track as a result of an earlier crash.

Reference: (https://en.wikipedia.org/wiki/1984_Dallas_Grand_Prix#Summary)

469.

An average-sized cat with its limbs extended achieves a terminal velocity of about 60 miles per hour, or 97 kilometers per hour, while an average-sized man reaches a terminal velocity of about 120 miles per hour, or 193 kilometers per hour. This helps make cats better than humans at surviving falls from great heights.

Reference: (http://www.bbc.com/news/magazine-17492802)

470.

In Rome, the strawberry was a symbol for Venus, the Goddess of Love, because of its heart shape and red color. Legend has it that if you break a double strawberry in half and share it with a member of the opposite sex, you will fall in love with each other.

Reference: (https://extension.illinois.edu/strawberries/history.cfm)

471.

The Chicxulub impactor, widely believed to be responsible for wiping out most dinosaurs, delivered an estimated impact energy of 10 billion Hiroshima A-bombs.

Reference: (https://en.wikipedia.org/wiki/Chicxulub_crater#Impact_specifics)

472.

There's a titanic snail called the achatina achatina, or African giant snail, that's bigger than your hand.

Reference: (https://en.wikipedia.org/wiki/Achatina_achatina#Description)

473.

An owner of The Hope Diamond pawned it in order to hire an investigator to track down the kidnappers of Charles Lindbergh's baby.

Reference: (https://www.thegreatcoursesdaily.com/curse-hope-diamond/)

474.

A scientist stationed in Antarctica managed to score a date through Tinder with a girl camping just 45 minutes away.

Reference: (https://www.thecut.com/2014/02/tinder-makes-its-first-match-in-antarctica.html)

475.

The guys who attempted to steal the British Crown Jewels flattened the Crown, cut the Scepter in two, and stuffed the Orb down their underwear.

Reference: (https://en.wikipedia.org/wiki/Thomas_Blood#Theft_of_the_Crown_Jewels)

476.

President Franklin D. Roosevelt was so enamored with postage stamps, he was known to draw rough sketches of the type of commemorative stamps he wanted the U.S. Postal Service to consider issuing.

Reference: (https://madoncollections.com/collectables/not-for-profit-clubs-societies/collectable-trivia/did-you-know/1118002-stamps)

477.

In 2010, psychologists found that pigeons outperformed college students on a variant of the Monty Hall problem, a famously vexing math puzzle. Unlike the birds, the humans, "failed to adopt optimal strategies, even with extensive training."

Reference: (https://undark.org/article/i-think-therefore-i-am-a-bird-on-animal-intelligence/)

478.

Inertia is a contronym and means both to resist movement and keep a steady state of movement depending on context.

Reference: (https://en.wikipedia.org/wiki/Inertia)

479.

Häagen-Dazs is a U.S. company that was founded in the Bronx. Its name was made up to be "Danish sounding" and convey "an aura of old world tradition and premium quality."

Reference: (https://en.wikipedia.org/wiki/H%C3%A4agen-Dazs)

480.

During the Nth Country Experiment, between the years 1964 and 1967, three recently graduated students managed to build an efficient nuclear bomb.

Reference: (https://en.wikipedia.org/wiki/Nth_Country_Experiment)

481.

There's a crime museum in Tennessee and they have a car owned by Ted Bundy, a car owned by John Dillinger and the Ford Bronco owned by O.J. Simpson.

Reference: (https://www.alcatrazeast.com/inside-alcatraz-east/)

482.

It took the stock market 25 years to recover from the 1929 crash.

Reference: (https://www.bloomberg.com/news/sponsors/cme-group/bitcoin-and-gold-a-growth-comparison/?adv=13162&prx_t=PzsDA-poXAUt8PA)

483.

Robert Landsburg was a photographer on Mount St. Helens as it erupted. Knowing he would not survive, he protected his film with his body and it was recovered and developed and provided valuable information to geologists.

Reference: (https://en.wikipedia.org/wiki/Robert_Landsburg)

484.

In 1970 California, psychedelic guru Timothy Leary was sentenced to ten years in prison for possession of two marijuana cigarette butts. After he was helped to escape from a minimum security prison, President Nixon labeled him as "the most dangerous man in America."

Reference: (http://countyourculture.com/2011/04/07/timothy-learys-escape-prison/)

485.

An innocent man, Lukis Anderson, was almost convicted for murder when his DNA was found in the murdered man in California.

Reference: (https://abcnews.go.com/amp/US/innocent-mans-dna-found-horrific-california-murder-scene/story?id=44098772)

486.

There was a special counsel appointed to investigate the finances of Jimmy Carter's family peanut business. After a year and a half, the investigation concluded in a 239 page report that there was no evidence that Carter had done anything illegal.

Reference: (https://en.wikipedia.org/wiki/Jimmy_Carter#Allegations_and_investigations)

487.

The mask in the Halloween movies is actually a mask of William Shatner's face spray painted white.

Reference: (https://www.snopes.com/fact-check/william-shatner-halloween-mask/)

488.

Almost all Rally Car drivers have a Co-Driver to assist with multiple aspects of the race.

Reference: (https://www.youtube.com/watch?v=JlAY-3-SoxE&feature=youtu.be)

489.

Color photography was invented in 1907 but was rarely used because of the complicated process needed to create colored photos.

Reference: (https://photography.tutsplus.com/articles/the-reception-of-color-photography-a-brief-history--cms-28333)

490.

In the 1990s, record label Sub Pop began all their rejection letters with "Dear Loser".

Reference: (http://www.lettersofnote.com/2011/09/dear-loser.html?m=1?a)

491.

Syphilis was the first "new" disease of the Columbian Exchange, newspapers covered its spread and scapegoated foreigners and deviants.

Reference: (https://en.wikipedia.org/wiki/History_of_syphilis)

492.

"Circular Breathing" was a technique used by players of wind instruments where you blow air out while also breathing in, giving a continuous note.

Reference: (https://en.wikipedia.org/wiki/Circular_breathing)

493.

The inventor of the Post-It Note, Dr. Spencer Silver, created the product by accident in an attempt to create a "stronger, tougher adhesive."

Reference: (https://www.post-it.com/3M/en_US/post-it/contact-us/about-us/)

494.

England was connected to Europe by land as recently as 20,000 years ago.

Reference: (https://youtu.be/4P9wQj6qX2I)

495.

There is a massive spending gap between students and university athletes, up 8 to 12 times as much at larger D-1 schools.

Reference: (https://www.hepinc.com/newsroom/state-universities-spending-over-100000-per-athlete-8-to-12-times-more-than-academics/)

496.

The 1970 song "25 or 6 to 4" by Chicago is about the clock reading either 3:35 or 3:34 AM as a musician tries to write songs late at night. The title was often thought to be about measuring out drug quantities.

Reference: (https://en.wikipedia.org/wiki/25_or_6_to_4)

497.

Chanel was accused of cultural appropriation for selling a $1325 boomerang.

Reference: (https://www.nytimes.com/2017/05/16/fashion/chanel-boomerang-cultural-appropriation.html)

498.

Satirical news site The Onion was almost "sued out of existence" in 1996 by Janet Jackson. The article that prompted the lawsuit was titled "Dying Boy Gets Wish: To Pork Janet Jackson."

Reference: (https://en.wikipedia.org/wiki/The_Onion#Madison_(1988%E2%80%932001))

499.

The most expensive hotel in the world is in New York and costs $100,000 per night.

Reference: (https://safehaven.com/article/45079/Billionaires-Only-The-Most-Exclusive-Hotels-In-The-World)

500.

The 1890s are considered the Golden Age of electric cars. They held the land speed record at the time and dominated the market until the 1920s when their 40 to 50 mile range was not suitable for the growing road system in the U.S.

Reference: (https://en.wikipedia.org/wiki/History_of_the_electric_vehicle)

501.

Cherries are a member of the Prunus genus which also includes almonds, peaches, plums, and apricots.

Reference: (https://en.wikipedia.org/wiki/Prunus)

502.

Sandra Bullock helped kickstart George Lopez's television career after watching his stand up. She was concerned with the lack of visibility of Latinos on American television and pitched the idea to Lopez to star and produce a show centered around him.

Reference: (https://www.nytimes.com/2002/11/27/arts/life-so-sad-he-had-be-funny-george-lopez-mines-rich-vein-gloom-with-all-latino.html)

503.

Some rosé wine is made from literally blending red wine and white wine together.

Reference: (https://www.getvinebox.com/blogs/learn/50-shades-of-rose-the-secret-sides-of-the-pinkish-wine)

504.

Dolphins have been observed sliding down whales.

Reference: (https://www.amnh.org/explore/science-bulletins/(watch)/bio/news/whales-give-dolphins-a-lift/)

505.

Shari Lewis, of Lambchop fame, wrote the original Star Trek episode "The Lights of Zetar."

Reference: (http://memory-alpha.wikia.com/wiki/Shari_Lewis)

506.

Yoko Ono created "Action Poems" instructing readers to make sandwiches and use blood for art.

Reference: (https://www.youtube.com/watch?v=Y5oTrDXCKAg)

507.

The Bortle Scale is a nine-point scale that measures the night sky's brightness in a given location based on celestial bodies being visible and light pollution preventing it.

Reference: (http://www.skyandtelescope.com/astronomy-resources/light-pollution-and-astronomy-the-bortle-dark-sky-scale/)

508.

Plastic bags are better for the environment: cotton bags needs 7,100 reuses to be better for the environment than 1 plastic bag.

Reference: (http://mst.dk/service/publikationer/publikationsarkiv/2018/mar/plastposer-lca/)

509.

During a training exercise, an F-106 fighter jet entered a flat spin, causing the pilot to bail out. Instead of crashing, the jet continued flying and landed on its belly in a field, only suffering minor damages.

Reference: (https://en.wikipedia.org/wiki/Cornfield_Bomber#History)

510.

The University of Pennsylvania has produced more billionaire undergrad alumni than any other college in the world. 25 current billionaires received their Bachelor's from the university, while Harvard has 22 undergrad alumni billionaires and Yale has 20.

Reference: (http://www.businessinsider.com/why-upenn-produces-so-many-billionaires-2014-10)

511.

A woman who was being held at knifepoint by her boyfriend got help from authorities by typing "911hostage help!" in the comments section of a Pizza Hut online order.

Reference: (https://www.cnn.com/2015/05/06/us/florida-pizza-order-saves-mom/index.html)

512.

The Boeing 777 flying Malaysia Airlines Flight 370, which disappeared mysteriously in 2014, was the 404th Boeing 777 manufactured.

Reference: (https://en.wikipedia.org/wiki/Malaysia_Airlines_Flight_370#Aircraft)

513.

In the 1800s, a cult leader gave 600 acres of land to God but the State of Pennsylvania took possession and sold it because the Almighty didn't pay His taxes.

Reference: (http://pabook2.libraries.psu.edu/palitmap/Celestia.html)

514.

The Tampa Bay Lightning may have been owned by the Japanese mafia via a shady entity called Kokusai Green.

Reference: (https://www.si.com/vault/1998/03/30/240924/team-turmoil-a-mystery-owner-squabbling-management-a-nine-figure-debt-and-a-rotten-record-have-put-the-tampa-bay-lightning-probably-the-worst-run-franchise-in-sports-on-the-brink-of-ruin)

515.

Christopher Nolan wanted to shoot the movie "Dunkirk" without a script. After telling his wife Emma Thomas and designer Nathan Crowley this, they convinced him to write an actual script that became the final film.

Reference: (https://www.hollywoodreporter.com/heat-vision/dunkirk-director-christopher-nolan-wanted-shoot-movie-script-1026790)

516.

28 of the 30 tallest statues in the world are Asian monuments to the Buddha or other spiritual figures. The other two are Soviet statues meant to honor its heroes of World War II.

Reference: (https://en.wikipedia.org/wiki/List_of_tallest_statues)

517.

Theodore Roosevelt as a child, watched Lincoln's funeral procession pass by his house. His admiration for Abe was reinforced later in life when he met John Hay, who was Abe's secretary. Hay gifted a ring that contained Lincoln's hair to Teddy. Teddy then wore the ring on his inauguration day.

Reference: (http://mentalfloss.com/article/27777/how-teddy-roosevelt-ended-abe-lincoln%E2%80%99s-hair)

518.

Strong odors, such as cologne and perfume, may cause a person's blood vessels to swell and dilate and, in turn, stimulate the nerve system in the brain associated with head pain causing headaches and migraines.

Reference: (https://wonderopolis.org/wonder/why-do-people-get-headaches-from-certain-scents)

519.

Scientists were able to predict a person's political orientation with 95 percent accuracy based solely on how their brain reacts to viewing disgusting, but non-political, images.

Reference: (http://research.vtc.vt.edu/news/2014/oct/29/liberal-or-conservative-brain-responses-disgusting/)

520.

Marrying a U.S. citizen doesn't grant citizenship; green card carrying spouses must cohabitate in marital union 3 years just to become eligible for application.

Reference: (https://www.uscis.gov/us-citizenship/citizenship-through-naturalization/naturalization-spouses-us-citizens)

521.

During World War II, the Italian army in North Africa accidently shot down the plane carrying their own commander, killing him.

Reference: (https://en.wikipedia.org/wiki/Italo_Balbo#Death)

522.

The Naruto no Uzushio whirlpools inspired the name for the manga character Uzumaki Naruto.

Reference: (https://en.wikipedia.org/wiki/Naruto_whirlpools)

523.

Ostriches are sexually aroused by humans.

Reference: (https://io9.gizmodo.com/5876033/that-ostrich-over-there-it-is-totally-into-you)

524.

The USPS and the U.S. Navy teamed up in an effort to deliver mail faster in 1959. Using a cruise missile with mail containers instead of warheads, the first "Missile Mail" hit its target in 22 minutes. The USPS officially established a branch and delivered 3,000 pieces of mail to Norfolk, Virginia.

Reference: (https://en.wikipedia.org/w/index.php?title=Rocket_mail#United_States)

525.

Japan has a national exercise routine and millions of people across Japan do the same routine at the same time.

Reference: (https://www.nippon.com/en/features/jg00068/)

526.

Operation Cone of Power is a "magical assault" on Adolf Hitler that was claimed to have stopped the amphibious invasion of Britain.

Reference: (http://mentalfloss.com/article/86145/operation-cone-power-when-british-witches-attacked-adolf-hitler)

527.

Wilhelm Stuckart was responsible for the Nazi regime's program of euthanasia for "deformed newborns." Two years after creating the laws, his own son born with Down syndrome became one of their victims.

Reference: (https://wikipedia.org/wiki/Wilhelm_Stuckart)

528.

In December 2000, a family in Japan was killed in their home. After killing the family, the murderer used the family computer, ate ice cream, used the bathroom, and left his pullover behind before leaving. Although the police has the suspect's DNA and a possible description, the case is unsolved.

Reference: (https://en.wikipedia.org/wiki/Setagaya_family_murder?wprov=sfla1#The_murders)

529.

Peanuts are not nuts, they grow underground, and are related to peas and beans.

Reference: (https://www.almanac.com/content/how-grow-your-own-peanuts)

530.

A writer for Futurama created a new math theorem to explain one of the show's plot twists.

Reference: (https://gizmodo.com/5618502/futurama-writer-invented-a-new-math-theorem-just-to-use-in-the-show)

531.

When helium is cooled to a few degrees below its boiling point, it will suddenly be able to do things that other fluids can't; such as, dribble through molecule-thin cracks, climb up and over the sides of a dish, and remain motionless when its container is spun due to its frictionless flow.

Reference: (https://www.scientificamerican.com/article/superfluid-can-climb-walls/)

532.

Phantom traffic jams, queues of traffic not caused by vehicle collisions or roadworks, are the result of a single driver braking suddenly, causing each successive car to break to a greater degree, creating a wave of stopped or slowed traffic.

Reference: (https://www.vox.com/2014/11/24/7276027/traffic-jam)

533.

Jimmy Page considers "Stairway to Heaven" a masterpiece. Robert Plant does not share his fondness. Plant has referred to it as a "wedding song" and insists that his favorite Led Zeppelin song is "Kashmir."

Reference: (http://www.songfacts.com/detail.php?id=328)

534.

When Michael Scott tries ordering "Gabagool" in an episode of "The Office", that word isn't completely wrong.

Reference: (https://www.atlasobscura.com/articles/how-capicola-became-gabagool-the-italian-new-jersey-accent-explained)

535.

The most visited museum in Scandinavia is a maritime museum dedicated to a single boat that sank in 1628.

Reference: (https://en.wikipedia.org/wiki/Vasa_Museum)

536.

Between 1925 and 1967, it was illegal in Tennessee for public school teachers to deny creationism.

Reference: (https://en.wikipedia.org/wiki/Butler_Act)

537.

When Josh Brolin was filming "Grindhouse," he had Quentin Tarantino direct and Robert Rodriguez shoot his audition tape for "No Country For Old Men." The Coen Brothers' response to the audition tape was, "Who lit it?"

Reference: (http://www.indiewire.com/2016/02/how-quentin-tarantino-robert-rodriguez-made-josh-brolins-no-country-for-old-men-audition-tape-83932/)

538.

Luxembourg, despite having a population of 600,000 people, has won the Eurovision Song Contest 5 times. None of their winners were even born in the country.

Reference:(https://en.wikipedia.org/wiki/Luxembourg_in_the_Eurovision_Song_Contest#Contestants)

539.

Where's Wally? is a British series of children's puzzles published in the U.S. and Canada as Where's Waldo?

Reference: (https://en.wikipedia.org/wiki/Where%27s_Wally%3F)

540.

The McGurk Effect is a perceptual phenomenon where visual perception changes what sound the viewer hears.

Reference: (https://www.youtube.com/watch?v=jtsfidRq2tw)

541.

Camels have an organ called dulla, which looks like testicles in their mouth, which they display to attract mates.

Reference: (http://www.digitaljournal.com/science/four-amazing-facts-to-know-about-camels/article/380661)

542.

Josh Brolin's stepmom is Barbra Streisand.

Reference: (https://en.wikipedia.org/wiki/Josh_Brolin#Early_life)

543.

There are more trees on Earth than stars in the Milky Way.

Reference: (https://www.worldatlas.com/articles/did-you-know-that-there-are-more-trees-on-earth-than-stars-in-the-milky-way.html)

544.

Henry Cavill missed the call from Zack Syder for the Superman role because he was playing World of Warcraft.

Reference: (https://www.youtube.com/watch?v=wmfFT2iORVg&feature=youtu.be&t=1m31s)

545.

Skunk is a non-lethal, strong-odored liquid used for crowd control by the Israel Defense Forces. When tested on a select group in India, the product failed miserably: "Those who can ignore the smell can drink the liquid also."

Reference: (https://en.wikipedia.org/wiki/Skunk_(weapon))

546.

The "Pioneering Spirit", the largest construction ship in the world and record holder for biggest offshore lift.

Reference: (https://en.wikipedia.org/wiki/Pioneering_Spirit_(ship))

547.

The U.S. Code of banking law clarifies that its use of the term "insane person" includes all idiots, lunatics, and person non-compos mentis.

Reference: (https://www.gpo.gov/fdsys/pkg/USCODE-2011-title1/pdf/USCODE-2011-title1.pdf)

548.

"Bouncing bombs" were used in World War II to destroy dams. Instead of being dropped above the dam, they were dropped above the lake then bounced on the water surface towards the target.

Reference: (https://en.wikipedia.org/wiki/Operation_Chastise)

549.

The Bronx Zoo had a human zoo exhibit in 1906. The attraction was a Congo Pygmy named Ota Benga.

Reference: (https://www.cnn.com/2015/06/03/opinions/newkirk-bronx-zoo-man-cage/index.html)

550.

Christopher Nolan says the scene he's most proud of out of his entire filmography is the opening plane scene in "The Dark Knight Rises."

Reference: (http://www.businessinsider.com/christopher-nolan-reveals-most-proud-of-the-dark-knight-rises-opening-scene-2015-4)

551.

For the first time since records began in 1880, young people aged 18 to 34 are more likely to live with their parents than a romantic partner.

Reference: (http://www.pewsocialtrends.org/2016/05/24/for-first-time-in-modern-era-living-with-parents-edges-out-other-living-arrangements-for-18-to-34-year-olds/)

552.

Rats laugh when you tickle them.

Reference:(https://www.youtube.com/attribution_link?a=oeuK7dpMM5M&u=%2Fwatch%3Fv%3Dj-admRGFVNM%26feature%3Dshare)

553.

A pile of trash reaching 45 meters altitude was named Mt. Cleese after the comedian John Cleese called the city the "suicide capital of New Zealand."

Reference: (https://teara.govt.nz/en/photograph/37117/mt-cleese)

554.

Adjusted for inflation, a VHS copy of "Back to the Future" from before 1986 was more expensive than a Blu-ray set of the entire trilogy in 2018.

Reference: (https://www.youtube.com/watch?v=6YLlt1JWpRA)

555.

It's unknown where the tomb of Archimedes is located today. The last known record of his tomb was in 75 BC, 137 years after Archimedes had died, when Cicero had found the tomb in a neglected condition and overgrown with bushes, and had the tomb cleaned up.

Reference: (https://en.wikipedia.org/wiki/Archimedes#Biography)

556.

Warren Buffett eats breakfast every day at McDonald's, never spends more than 3.17$ and buys the cheap meal on days when the markets are down.

Reference: (https://www.cnbc.com/2017/01/30/warren-buffetts-breakfast-never-costs-more-than-317.html)

557.

The Akashi Kaikyō suspension bridge in Japan experienced a 7.2 magnitude earthquake whilst still under construction. The resulting ground shift pushed the bridge's two supporting towers apart meaning an extra 1 meter had to be added to the main span, which is currently the longest in the world.

Reference: (https://www.youtube.com/watch?v=FuWM6-xOQCY&t=0s)

558.

Canadian Prime Minister R.B. Bennett lived in a luxurious 17-room hotel suite in Ottawa for the duration of his time in office between 1930 to 1935. It was during the Great Depression and his government lost when news of his expensive lifestyle became public.

Reference: (http://www.rideautownshiphistory.org/presentation%20oct%2015.htm)

559.

The "Bisley Boy"'" conspiracy theory states that the reason Elizabeth I never married, wore heavy makeup and went bald was because she was actually a boy who had been cradle-swapped with the real princess after she died.

Reference: (http://www.elizabethfiles.com/the-bisley-boy/3255/)

560.

There is a variant of the traveling salesman problem in which the routes are unknown until the graph is explored. It's called the Canadian traveler problem, named so because of the difficulty Canadians have traveling when it snows.

Reference: (https://en.wikipedia.org/wiki/Canadian_traveller_problem)

561.

The Sun is white, but it can often appear yellow, orange or red through Earth's atmosphere due to atmospheric Rayleigh scattering.

Reference: (https://en.wikipedia.org/wiki/G-type_main-sequence_star)

562.

Canada has a series of grand railway hotels across the country. Each five star hotel was originally built by the Canadian railway companies, designed to serve the passengers of the country's then expanding rail network.

Reference: (https://en.wikipedia.org/wiki/Canada%27s_grand_railway_hotels)

563.

A group of embittered singles in Shanghai purchased all odd-numbered cinema seats forcing couples to sit apart on Valentine's Day.

Reference: (https://www.theguardian.com/lifeandstyle/2014/feb/14/valentines-day-odd-numbered-cinema-seats-china)

564.

Olympic athlete Carl Lewis was drafted in the 1984 NFL and NBA drafts.

Reference: (https://www.nfldraftdiamonds.com/in-1984-track-star-carl-lewis-was-drafted-by-the-nba-and-nfl/)

565.

There are over 12,000 different species of millipedes and there's a lab in the United States that only studies this arthropods.

Reference: (https://www.atlasobscura.com/articles/up-close-only-millipede-lab-united-states-entomology-appalachians)

566.

Prince was directly inspired to write Purple Rain by the success of Bob Seger.

Reference: (https://www.npr.org/2014/12/06/368508262/all-possibilities-the-purple-rain-story)

567.

ESports was acknowledged as a sporting activity by the International Olympic Committee in 2017.

Reference: (https://en.wikipedia.org/wiki/ESports#Olympic_Games_recognizition)

568.

Ancient China knew about the Roman Empire. They called them "Daqin" and documented several things concerning them, including a guide on how to reach them from China.

Reference: (https://io9.gizmodo.com/heres-what-third-century-china-thought-about-the-roman-1253007513/amp)

569.

In 1911, the Mona Lisa was stolen from the Louvre Museum in Paris, and Pablo Picasso was one of the suspects.

Reference: (https://www.npr.org/2011/07/30/138800110/the-theft-that-made-the-mona-lisa-a-masterpiece)

570.

A colony of narcoleptic dogs was maintained for 20 years by Stanford University which bred 669 dogs to better understand the disorder. "Bear", the last dog in the colony died in 2014.

Reference: (https://www.ncbi.nlm.nih.gov/pubmed/9481825)

571.

Jimmy Carter was the first U.S. president to be born in a hospital.

Reference: (http://www.american-presidents-history.com/presidential-firsts.html)

572.

The basis for McDonald's Big Mac sauce, Thousand Island dressing, is Canadian.

Reference: (https://en.wikipedia.org/wiki/Thousand_Island_dressing)

573.

"Kaiser", the German word for emperor, is directly derived from the Roman emperor's title of Caesar. In Latin, every "c" is pronounced like "k" and never as "s".

Reference: (https://en.wikipedia.org/wiki/Kaiser)

574.

The volume of the nucleus could fit into the volume of its atom 2,580,000,000,000,000 times.

Reference: (https://en.wikipedia.org/wiki/Atomic_radius)

575.

A woman accidentally left a dildo inside herself for 10 years.

Reference: (http://www.news.com.au/lifestyle/relationships/sex/surgeons-remove-toy-stuck-in-womans-vagina-for-10-years/news-story/08e218b3689635bc88794a1a0cd718b5)

576.

Archie Mitchell, the husband and father of the only civilian World War II casualties on the continental U.S., was kidnapped by the Viet Cong in 1962 and has not been seen since.

Reference: (https://en.wikipedia.org/wiki/Archie_E._Mitchell)

577.

The feeling of stepping on a stopped escalator is a psychological effect called "The Broken Escalator Phenomenon" and is our brains expecting it to be moving even when we know it's not.

Reference: (https://wikipedia.org/wiki/Broken_escalator_phenomenon#)

578.

Susan Backlinie was a stuntwoman, animal trainer, and also appeared in her own softcore porn pictorial in Penthouse magazine.

Reference: (https://en.wikipedia.org/wiki/Susan_Backlinie)

579.

"Thing" from the Addams Family has a full name: "Thing T. Thing."

Reference: (https://en.wikipedia.org/wiki/Thing_(The_Addams_Family))

580.

A Los Angeles City Councilmember for Holmby Hills wants to add the Playboy Mansion to the city's roster of historic-cultural landmarks, citing the mansion's architecture—an "excellent example of a Gothic-Tudor" and connection to the neighborhood's history.

Reference: (https://la.curbed.com/2017/11/8/16622566/playboy-mansion-la-historic-cultural-landmark)

581.

May 2018 falls as an extra special month according to Hindus, and is celebrated as "Adhik Mass" due to a gap between lunar and solar calendars that only occurs every 3 years.

Reference: (https://en.wikipedia.org/wiki/Adhik_Maas)

582.

The idea for the backwards "R" in KoRn's logo came from Toys'R'Us, where many of the band's members previously worked.

Reference: (https://en.wikipedia.org/wiki/Korn)

583.

Shaun White was mentored by Tony Hawk.

Reference: (http://www.latimes.com/sports/olympics/la-sp-olympics-shaun-white-future-20180215-story.html)

584.

Nearly a quarter of Russians don't know who Karl Marx was.

Reference: (https://themoscowtimes.com/articles/marx-at-soviet-union-godfather-all-but-forgotten-russia-61359?amp)

585.

The Neil Armstrong Air and Space Museum in Ohio is shaped like a Moon and it features the Gemini VIII spacecraft, Neil Armstrong's Gemini and Apollo spacesuits, and a lunar sample. The museum has no formal relationship with Armstrong.

Reference: (https://en.wikipedia.org/wiki/Armstrong_Air_and_Space_Museum)

586.

"The Stacks" in "Ready Player One" were actually a reality in Minnesota until they were deemed too ugly to survive and were torn down.

Reference: (https://99percentinvisible.org/article/mobile-home-skyscrapers-elusive-dream-vertical-urban-trailer-parks/)

587.

Japan had its own version of "The Price is Right" called "The Chance!" that featured the pop group Pink Lady. It aired from 1979 to 1986.

Reference: (https://www.youtube.com/watch?v=XQhMyQxmbrU)

588.

Miley Cyrus' first job was to pick up the bras and underwear from her dad's tour stage that his fans would throw and she got paid $10 for it.

Reference: (http://www.boomsbeat.com/articles/141/20140123/50-interesting-facts-about-miley-cyrus.htm)

589.

The World Record for the fastest growing plant belongs to a certain species of bamboo. They have been found to grow up to 35 inches per day at a rate of 0.00002 MPH. That's nearly 1.5 inches an hour. You could literally watch bamboo grow before your eyes.

Reference: (http://www.guinnessworldrecords.com/world-records/fastest-growing-plant/)

590.

Chuck Berry's home in St. Louis is included on the National Register of Historic Places in 2008 but it had badly deteriorated. The proposed Chuck Berry Cultural District by the community would be a lifeline to a dying and depopulating neighborhood.

Reference: (https://savingplaces.org/stories/around-and-around-st-louis-community-restore-chuck-berry-house#.Wvzif4gvzD4)

591.

Scientists recently discovered a super volcano under Antarctica, and although they believe it is of similar scale as Yellowstone, uncertainty remains as to the consequences of a potential eruption.

Reference: (http://www.newsweek.com/antarctica-melting-below-mantle-plume-almost-hot-yellowstone-supervolcano-705086)

592.

President Lyndon B. Johnson lost the election for his first term in Senate, but cheated out 20,000 votes. When that wasn't enough he "found" 202 votes 6 days after polls closed. He stooped investigation into it and held his seat.

Reference: (https://www.nytimes.com/1990/02/11/us/how-johnson-won-election-he-d-lost.html)

593.

During the Cold War, Nikita Khrushchev said to Mao Zedong that, "Berlin is the testicles of the West. Every time I want to make the West scream, I squeeze on Berlin."

Reference:(https://en.wikipedia.org/w/index.php?title=Cold_War#Berlin_ultimatum_and_European_integration)

594.

Richard Armitage threatened to bomb Pakistan "back to the Stone Age" if it didn't cooperate with U.S. in its efforts to defeat Taliban in Afghanistan. Pakistan, eventually, folded under pressure.

Reference: (http://www.rediff.com/news/2006/sep/22mush.htm)

595.

OPEC has essentially begged Russia to join the oil cartel twice.

Reference: (https://www.fool.com/investing/2017/03/29/why-isnt-russia-a-part-of-opec.aspx)

596.

Hunting in Niger has been banned since 1974 and one of its major parks is called W National Park, named after a bend in the Niger River. Home to the giraffe, it is reported to be last surviving population of the West African race.

Reference: (https://en.wikipedia.org/wiki/Wildlife_of_Niger)

597.

You have to earn more than $3 an hour extra at a real job to equal Uber driving due to the big tax deduction on mileage.

Reference: (https://therideshareguy.com/how-to-calculate-per-mile-earnings-instead-of-per-hour/)

598.

The name "orchid" derives from orchis, the Greek word for "testicle".

Reference: (https://en.wikipedia.org/wiki/Orchidaceae)

599.

"Kayfabe" is a slang term in professional wrestling used to describe the fact that it is a staged event, not a competitive sport, despite being presented as such; and that wrestlers, unlike actors who only portray their characters when on set or on stage, stay "in character" outside the shows.

Reference: (https://en.wikipedia.org/wiki/Kayfabe)

600.

"War of the Worlds" was inspired in part by the near complete extermination of Australian Tasmanian Aborigines following British colonization in the 1800s.

Reference: (http://www.indigilab.com.au/future-science/4643/)

601.

The Pentagon has an actual defense strategy for a zombie apocalypse. The document is known as CONPLAN 8888 and is a detailed guide on how to survive and fight against multiple types of zombies.

Reference: (http://documents.theblackvault.com/documents/controversies/FOIA16-041.pdf)

602.

167 people won their bet that Luis Suarez would bite someone in the World Cup in 2014.

Reference: (http://time.com/money/2921282/luis-suarez-bite-bet-worl/)

603.

The holes on a Bic pen cap are there to prevent the cap from completely obstructing the airway if accidently inhaled.

Reference: (https://www.bicworld.com/en/faq#accordion-item-386)

604.

In the early 1970s, the U.S. spent the equivalent of $20 billion on a military missile base that was closed after just 4 months.

Reference: (http://www.ghostsofnorthdakota.com/2011/08/14/nekoma-safeguard-complex/)

605.

A typo stopped a billion dollar bank heist from the Federal Reserve.

Reference: (https://www.reuters.com/article/us-usa-fed-bangladesh-typo-insight-idUSKCN0WC0TC)

606.

In 2012, more than 1 in 5 Americans were on some form of government assistance program.

Reference: (https://www.census.gov/newsroom/press-releases/2015/cb15-97.html)

607.

In 2017, an off-duty police officer dressed up as Batman was entertaining kids sick with cancer at a hospital. Coincidentally, as he left the hospital he caught and arrested a man who was attempting to steal multiple DVDs, including the Lego Batman Movie.

Reference: (http://kdvr.com/2017/06/21/off-duty-cop-dressed-as-batman-busts-shoplifter-taking-lego-batman-movie/)

608.

Kendrick Lamar is named after one of the founding members of The Temptations.

Reference: (http://www.xxlmag.com/news/2013/09/know-kendrick-lamar-named-one-temptations/)

609.

Howard Hughes was an insomniac and was frustrated that there was nothing good on TV late at night, so he bought a TV station and had it play his favorite movies 24/7.

Reference: (https://lasvegassun.com/news/2008/may/15/how-vegas-went-mob-corporate/)

610.

Peanuts creator Charles M. Schulz's first publication of artwork was published by Robert Ripley of Ripley's Believe It or Not! It was a cartoon of Schulz's dog Spike which later became the model for Peanuts' Snoopy.

Reference:(https://en.wikipedia.org/wiki/Ripley%27s_Believe_It_or_Not!#Syndicated_feature_panel)

611.

A U.S. Coast Guard cutter which once conducted combat missions in the Vietnam War was later transferred to the Vietnamese Coast Guard.

Reference: (https://en.wikipedia.org/wiki/USCGC_Morgenthau_(WHEC-722))

612.

One of the mint plant's first known uses in Europe was as a room deodorizer. The herb was strewn across floors to cover smells since stepping on the mint helped to spread its scent through the room.

Reference: (https://en.wikipedia.org/wiki/Mentha#Room_scent_and_aromatherapy)

613.

A woman scratched an itch, all the way through her skull and into her brain.

Reference: (https://www.newyorker.com/magazine/2008/06/30/the-itch)

614.

The Curse of Tippecanoe was a curse from the Shawnee tribe bestowed upon subsequent American presidents. William H. Harrison, who fought the Shawnee in at the Battle of Tippecanoe in 1811, was the first of series of presidents to die or be assassinated in office.

Reference: (https://en.wikipedia.org/wiki/Curse_of_Tippecanoe)

615.

Whiptail Lizards are a species without any males, only females.

Reference: (https://www.scientificamerican.com/article/asexual-lizards/)

616.

Grasshoppers and locusts are the same bug.

Reference: (https://www.reddit.com/user/Celtic134)

617.

If you are ejected into space, by immediately breathing out it is possible to survive for two minutes without permanent injury.

Reference: (https://www.cnet.com/g00/news/what-happens-to-the-unprotected-human-body-in-space/?i10c.encReferrer=&i10c.ua=1&i10c.dv=14)

618.

There was a singing competition where the contestants thought they were competing for best singer but were actually being judged to find the worst singer in America.

Reference: (https://en.wikipedia.org/wiki/Superstar_USA)

619.

Han van Meegeren was a Dutch painter. Master artist and con-artist, he forged paintings in the style of Johannes Vermeer, fooling curators for years. Despite his crimes, he is celebrated now as a World War II hero for selling counterfeit artwork to Nazi Reichsmarschall Hermann Göring.

Reference: (https://en.wikipedia.org/wiki/Han_van_Meegeren)

620.

In 1978, Sam Sloan, a man with no formal legal training, sued the U.S. Securities & Exchange Commission and argued his own case in front of the Supreme Court, winning it 9-0.

Reference: (https://en.wikipedia.org/wiki/Sam_Sloan)

621.

There was a scrapped hand drawn animated crossover short that would have brought together female Disney characters in a boarding school. Concept art was made and Alan Menken was on board, but never happened due to Disney focusing on digital animation and problems between the directors.

Reference: (https://www.dailydot.com/parsec/disney-princess-academy-david-kawena-oliver-ciappa/)

622.

There was a town in New Jersey called Nixon, which was destroyed in 1924 because of an explosion of the Ammonite building, one of the plants of the Nixon Nitration Works leased to Ammonite Company at the time, killing 20, destroying 40 houses and injuring a hundred people.

Reference: (http://www.rarenewspapers.com/view/648367)

623.

The Great Disappointment is the reaction that followed after Baptist preacher William Miller had wrongly proclaimed that Jesus would return to Earth on October 22nd, 1844. One Millerite later recalled: "I lay prostrate for 2 days without any pain – sick with disappointment."

Reference: (https://en.wikipedia.org/wiki/Great_Disappointment)

624.

In 2007, fans of the then-cancelled TV show "Jericho" sent more than 18,000 pounds of peanuts to CBS offices in a successful effort to save the show.

Reference: (https://www.cbsnews.com/news/jericho-fans-go-nuts/)

625.

The logo for Game Boy Color spelled out the word "COLOR" in the five original colors in which the unit was manufactured. They were Berry (C) Grape (O) Kiwi (L) Dandelion (O) Teal (R).

Reference: (https://en.wikipedia.org/wiki/Game_Boy_Color)

626.

Italians are snorting so much cocaine that their tainted urine is contaminating the Po River.

Reference: (https://ehjournal.biomedcentral.com/articles/10.1186/1476-069X-4-14)

627.

20% of the world's population speaks English.

Reference: (https://www.babbel.com/en/magazine/how-many-people-speak-english-and-where-is-it-spoken/)

628.

At the time of A Momentary Lapse of Reason tour, Roger Waters issued a writ for copyright fees for the band's use of the flying pig. Pink Floyd responded by attaching a large set of male genitalia to its underside to distinguish it from Waters' design.

Reference: (https://en.wikipedia.org/wiki/Pink_Floyd#A_Momentary_Lapse_of_Reason)

629.

ABC's Monday Night Football was the first national broadcast to announce the shooting of John Lennon.

Reference: (https://en.wikipedia.org/wiki/Monday_Night_Football#As_entertainment)

630.

Seals are able to understand rhythm and can bop their heads to music.

Reference: (https://youtu.be/6yS6qU_w3JQ)

631.

Too much added sugar can be one of the greatest threats to cardiovascular disease. Basically, the higher the intake of added sugar, the higher the risk for heart disease.

Reference: (https://www.health.harvard.edu/heart-health/the-sweet-danger-of-sugar)

632.

Male squirrels deposit secretions into a female squirrels' vagina that later harden into a plug or glues the tract together. Female tree squirrels sometimes manually remove the plug and either discard or consume it, thus enabling insemination by subsequent suitors.

Reference:(https://www.researchgate.net/publication/273287212_Removal_of_Copulatory_Plugs_by_Female_Tree_Squirrels)

633.

Many Venezuelan's turned to farming Runescape gold for a living as a result of economic difficulties.

Reference: (https://www.polygon.com/2017/9/10/16283926/venezuelan-gold-farming-runescape-targets)

634.

There's a critically endangered species of plant called the "pokemeboy".

Reference: (http://www.iucnredlist.org/details/43894/0)

635.

The Indian muntjac has the fewest chromosomes of any mammal, with 6 chromosomes for females and 7 for males.

Reference: (https://en.wikipedia.org/wiki/Indian_muntjac#Evolution_and_genetics)

636.

The Catacombs in Paris are a network of old caves, quarries and tunnels stretching hundreds of miles, and seemingly lined with bones of 12 million people.

Reference: (https://www.valdastravelvideo.com/2017/12/catacombs-of-paris-france.html)

637.

A 15 year old Ray Kroc lied about his age during World War I and became a Red Cross ambulance driver. In Kroc's Red Cross Company, there was another boy who lied about his age to get in; his name was Walt Disney.

Reference: (https://en.wikipedia.org/wiki/Ray_Kroc)

638.

The first photographs of the far side of the Moon were taken by Soviet "Luna-III" in 1959. The film used was taken from American spy balloons that were shot down over Russia by anti-aircraft gunners.

Reference: (http://www.svengrahn.pp.se/trackind/luna3/SpyBalloon.htm)

639.

In 2012, South Korea launched an initiative to reverse the trend of suicides on the Mapo Bridge called the Bridge of Life Project. The opposite occurred. The number of suicides at Mapo Bridge has increased by more than six fold since the beginning of the program.

Reference: (https://soranews24.com/2014/02/26/seoul-anti-suicide-initiative-backfires-deaths-increase-over-than-six-times/)

640.

An independent Yucatan Peninsula asked President James K. Polk to be annexed to the United States, but the annexation was declined by the senate.

Reference: (https://en.wikipedia.org/wiki/Republic_of_Yucat%C3%A1n#In_fiction)

641.

Joel Silver, producer of the "Matrix" and "Lethal Weapon," helped create Ultimate Frisbee in 1968.

Reference:(https://www.usultimate.org/about/history/hall_of_fame/founders_class_of_2005.aspx)

642.

During Johnson's administration, the Lyndon B. Johnson Ranch was known as the "Texas White House" because the President spent approximately 20% of his time in office there.

Reference: (https://en.wikipedia.org/wiki/Lyndon_B._Johnson_National_Historical_Park)

643.

Only one football match was ever played between footballing giants West Germany and the weaker East Germany; it was in Hamburg at the 1974 World Cup and the East won 1-0.

Reference: (https://www.tagesspiegel.de/sport/juergen-sparwasser-erinnert-sich-als-die-ddr-die-brd-bei-der-wm-1974-besiegte/10080542.htmll)

644.

It is a misdemeanor to paint someone's home in California, without working under a licensed painting contractor for 4 years at the journeyman level.

Reference:(http://www.cslb.ca.gov/Contractors/Applicants/Contractors_License/Exam_Application/Before_Applying_For_License.aspx)

645.

In 2007, Russia planted their national flag underwater in hopes of securing the Arctic's potential natural resources. "This isn't the 15th century," one foreign minister said. "You can't go around the world and just plant flags and say, 'We're claiming this territory.'"

Reference: (https://www.nytimes.com/2007/08/03/world/europe/03arctic.html)

646.

Colonial Lagos, Nigeria was a busy, cosmopolitan port. Its architecture was in both Victorian and Brazilian style, as many of the black elite were English-speakers from Sierra Leone and freedmen repatriated from Brazil and Cuba. Africans also were represented on the Lagos Legislative Council.

Reference: (https://en.wikipedia.org/wiki/Colonial_Nigeria)

647.

Blink 182 frontman Tom DeLonge left the band to form a group to search for aliens and explore the outer edges of science. He has since recruited scientists and ex-government officials including the official who ran the U.S.'s secret government program to find UFOs.

Reference: (https://www.vox.com/2017/12/16/16785122/ufos-harry-reid-pentagon-defense-blink-182)

648.

Nearly half of U.S. counties don't have a practicing obstetrician-gynecologist.

Reference: (https://www.npr.org/2018/02/22/587953272/does-a-larger-role-for-midwives-mean-better-care)

649.

McDonalds had implemented bubble gum flavored broccoli in an attempt to get kids healthier.

Reference: (http://www.businessinsider.com/mcdonalds-bubble-gum-broccoli-2014-11)

650.

Sandwich day and housewife day are celebrated on the same date, which is the 3rd of November.

Reference: (https://nationaldaycalendar.com/national-housewifes-day-november-3/%20https://nationaldaycalendar.com/national-sandwich-day-november-3/)

651.

Taking office the day before his 40th birthday, Joe Clark is the youngest person to become Canadian Prime Minister. He represented Canada internationally at the G7 summit and had a good relationship with Jimmy Carter.

Reference: (https://en.wikipedia.org/wiki/Joe_Clark)

652.

In 1976, a group of scientists led by Leon Lederman thought they had discovered a particle called the Upsilon meson. Upon further tests, they realized they made a mistake, and that the particle did not really exist. They later called this "discovery" the Oops-Leon, a pun on Upsilon and Leon.

Reference: (https://en.wikipedia.org/wiki/Oops-Leon)

653.

In March 2005, Tori Alamaze released "Don't Cha" as her debut single. The song failed and she was dropped. In April 2005, CeeLo Green gave the song to The Pussycat Dolls. They released it as their debut single, and the song reached No. 2 on Billboard, and sold more than 6 million copies worldwide.

Reference: (https://en.wikipedia.org/wiki/Don%27t_Cha)

654.

In 2005, Mr. Graham Pendrill, 57, visited Maasai Mara and met the Maasai. He loved their lifestyle so much that he sold his 1.2 million dollar mansion so that he could move to Kenya and be proclaimed as the elder of a Maasai tribe. ☐ ☐

Reference: (http://allafrica.com/stories/200508291242.html)

655.

The Great Gatsby was almost titled "Trimalchio in West Egg," based on an ancient Roman fictional ex-slave who came into money and threw lavish parties, but the author's wife and publisher convinced him to call it The Great Gatsby.

Reference: (https://en.wikipedia.org/wiki/The_Great_Gatsby#Title)

656.

Pets who ingest anti-freeze can be given vodka drips as treatment.

Reference: (https://www.petmd.com/news/health-science/cat-saved-antifreeze-poisoning-vodka-36156)

657.

A Florida woman was run over by her own car when she tried to escape a cat that attacked her through her open car window.

Reference: (https://www.cbsnews.com/news/cat-attack-woman-run-over-car-cocoa-beach-florida/)

658.

Adultery is considered a felony punishable by a $10 to $500 dollar fine or 4 years in prison in New York, Massachusetts, Idaho, Oklahoma, Michigan, South Carolina, and Wisconsin.

Reference: (https://www.freep.com/story/life/family/2014/04/17/in-which-states-is-cheating-on-your-spouse-illegal/28936155/)

659.

"Groaning Beer" is made for mothers in labor to drink, to bathe newborns in, and for the fathers to get drunk enough to drown out the sounds of childbirth.

Reference: (https://www.theatlantic.com/business/archive/2013/11/women-and-beer-a-4-500-year-history-is-coming-full-circle/281338/)

660.

The Soviet Union has sold Iran dolphins that had been trained to kill.

Reference: (http://news.bbc.co.uk/2/hi/world/middle_east/670551.stm)

661.

Spiders have blue blood because in spiders oxygen is bound to hemocyanin, a molecule that contains copper instead of iron as in humans.

Reference: (http://mediabunny.com/20-spider-facts-you-did-not-know-about/2018)

662.

The Philadelphia Phillies are the oldest continuous, one-name, one-city franchise in all of professional American sports, dating back to 1883.

Reference: (https://en.wikipedia.org/wiki/Philadelphia_Phillies)

663.

After the first attempt to assassinate Franz Ferdinand failed due to a mistimed bomb, the assassin swallowed a cyanide pill and jumped into the Miljacka River to kill himself. The pill was expired and only induced vomiting and the Miljacka was only 13 centimeters deep due to the hot, dry summer.

Reference:(https://en.wikipedia.org/wiki/Assassination_of_Archduke_Franz_Ferdinand#Bombing)

664.

Dedovshchina is a hazing ritual and the practical enslavement of Russian conscript soldiers by their superiors and supervisors.

Reference: (https://www.hrw.org/report/2004/10/19/wrongs-passage/inhuman-and-degrading-treatment-new-recruits-russian-armed-forces)

665.

St. Petersburg is considered the most European city in Russia and many tourists there don't go anywhere else as the city has more relaxed visa rules than the rest of the country. It is an entirely "different landscape" only 100 kilometers away.

Reference: (https://www.npr.org/2010/08/26/129435807/st-petersburg-a-glimpse-of-what-russia-is-not)

666.

NOKIA, before shifting to a consumer electronics company, was producing rubber boots.

Reference: (http://bgr.com/2014/07/01/nokia-future-analysis-smart-shoes/)

667.

In 1977, Francis Coppola wrote to John Lennon about contributing to "Apocalypse Now" and Lennon replied.

Reference: (http://faroutmagazine.co.uk/that-time-francis-coppola-wrote-to-john-lennon-about-contributing-to-apocalypse-now-1977/)

668.

"Get Your War On", is a comic that circulated the Internet in the days after 9/11. It was made entirely out of a handful of "very crude" workplace clip art frames, in which several jaded characters react to the country's thirst for war.

Reference: (https://en.wikipedia.org/wiki/Get_Your_War_On)

669.

At the age of 17, Srinivasa Ramanujan had developed Bernoulli numbers and calculated Euler's constant up to 15 decimal places.

Reference: (https://www.nytimes.com/1987/07/14/science/an-isolated-genius-is-given-his-due.html)

670.

President Kennedy's family repurchased the house where he was born in after his assassination. His mother restored the house to her recollection of its 1917 appearance and wanted to restore the home to the hour of his birth. She donated the home to the National Park Service in 1967.

Reference: (https://en.wikipedia.org/wiki/John_Fitzgerald_Kennedy_National_Historic_Site)

671.

There is a UFO exhibit in a town in Alberta, Canada where you can view actual photographs of UFOs, crop circles and cattle mutilations. It has the first official UFO landing pad.

Reference: (http://www.town.stpaul.ab.ca/UFO-Landing-Pad)

672.

Hans Christian Andersen was so terrified of being buried alive, he made a practice of leaving a note, "I only appear to be dead," on his bedside table while he slept.

Reference: (http://buffalonews.com/adblock/)

673.

John von Neumann, generally regarded as the foremost mathematician of his time, frequently drove while reading a book resulting in numerous accidents and tickets. When he was employed as a consultant for IBM, fellow coworker Cuthbert Hurd would pay for the tickets.

Reference: (https://en.wikipedia.org/wiki/John_von_Neumann)

674.

An English novelist visited Chesil beach and kept a few pebbles for writing inspiration. This area is part of a UNESCO protected site with much scientific importance. He confessed of the crime on a British radio show in 2007 and returned the shingles after facing a fine and public outcry.

Reference: (https://www.theguardian.com/uk/2007/apr/06/books.booksnews)

675.

Betsy Aardsma was a graduate student who was stabbed at the Penn State University library. Because the wound was so small and the fact that she was wearing a red dress, no one noticed that she was stabbed until after she died, and EMTs thought she was suffering a seizure. The case is unsolved.

Reference: (https://en.wikipedia.org/wiki/Murder_of_Betsy_Aardsma#Murder)

676.

Although Brigham Young neither ordered nor approved the Mountain Meadows Massacre, an attack by Mormons, disguised as Indians, that wiped out an entire wagon train of 120 non-Mormon men, women and children, he did condone the attack afterward.

Reference: (http://archive.sltrib.com/article.php?id=2961537&itype=CMSID)

677.

Ramin Djawadi, the composer for Game of Thrones, has the sensory condition Synesthesia, which allows him to visualize and associate music with color.

Reference: (https://youtu.be/3Sj99Pc4q8c)

678.

Unlike 10 Downing Street or the White House, 24 Sussex is used almost exclusively as a place of residence by the Canadian Prime Minister. A Prime Minister's wife has said the residence is "completely lacking" in architectural value and is not worth saving.

Reference: (https://en.wikipedia.org/wiki/24_Sussex_Drive)

679.

Lemmy Kilmister of Motorhead stole his first bass guitar and learned how to play while onstage with his earlier band, Hawkwind.

Reference: (http://www.notreble.com/buzz/2010/12/16/lemmy-reveals-how-he-started-playing-bass/)

680.

Astronaut Luca Parmitano almost drowned in space when the water cooling system started leaking. This prompted NASA to add pads in the helmet that can absorb roughly 1.5 liters of liquid.

Reference: (https://www.youtube.com/watch?v=jWPxkB7GaBQ&feature=youtu.be)

681.

The Pilgrims only landed at Plymouth Rock because they ran out of beer.

Reference: (https://history.howstuffworks.com/history-vs-myth/settlers-plymouth-rock-out-beer.htm)

682.

The first birth control pill used Puerto Rican women as guinea pigs for their clinical trials.

Reference: (https://www.history.com/news/birth-control-pill-history-puerto-rico-enovid)

683.

Cattle and deer all over the world tend to align themselves with Earth's magnetic field. Both types of animals appear to graze in a north-south direction that aligns with magnetic north.

Reference: (https://news.nationalgeographic.com/news/2008/08/080825-magnetic-cows.html)

684.

Files kept secret for 60 years indicate British intelligence may have knowingly sent more than 50 of its own agents to almost certain death in occupied Holland during the Second World War as part of a complicated "double double agent" game played against the Germans.

Reference: (https://www.telegraph.co.uk/news/uknews/1469303/Did-British-intelligence-send-its-own-spies-to-their-deaths.html)

685.

The average human body temperature is not 98.6° Fahrenheit it's 98.2° Fahrenheit and it's different for everyone.

Reference:(https://www.realclearscience.com/blog/2015/08/the_average_body_temperature_is_not_986_degrees.html)

686.

After the 1980 film "Popeye" flopped, the set was abandoned, so the locals of Mellieha, Malta reclaimed it as a Popeye theme park.

Reference: (https://www.atlasobscura.com/places/popeye-s-village)

687.

Sweden uses submarines powered by Sterling engines, which are quieter than both internal combustion and nuclear engines, and they managed to sink a fully escorted U.S. aircraft carrier in simulated wargames.

Reference: (https://en.wikipedia.org/wiki/Gotland-class_submarine)

688.

A Belgian named George Washington invented a process that allowed instant coffee to be mass produced.

Reference: (https://en.wikipedia.org/wiki/George_Washington_(inventor))

689.

Astronomers believe our home galaxy, the Milky Way, has a supermassive black hole, which is many times larger than a regular black hole.

Reference: (https://en.wikipedia.org/wiki/Sagittarius_A)

690.

New York City is the most linguistically diverse city in the world, with 800 languages spoken.

Reference: (https://www.nytimes.com/2010/04/29/nyregion/29lost.html)

691.

The Tunguska event is an asteroid "impact" that took place in Siberia in 1908. Early estimates suggested that upwards 15 megatons of energy were released, but there were no confirmed fatalities.

Reference: (https://en.wikipedia.org/wiki/Tunguska_event)

692.

Researchers in South Korea studied 10,711 adults and found that women who ate instant noodles at least twice a week were 68 percent more likely to have metabolic syndrome. The effect was not apparent in men.

Reference: (https://well.blogs.nytimes.com/2014/08/20/instant-noodles-tied-to-heart-risk/)

693.

The father of Metallica's Lars Ulrich, Torben Ulrich, was a professional tennis player that competed for the Danish Davis Cup team.

Reference: (https://en.wikipedia.org/wiki/Torben_Ulrich)

694.

Romans may have invented the burger, called Isicia Omentata, over 1,500 years ago which was made with minced meat, pepper, wine, pine nuts and a rich fish-based sauce called garum. The Romans also introduced the first fast food restaurants, called a thermopolium, which sold hot ready-to-eat food.

Reference: (https://museumcrush.org/the-1500-year-old-recipe-that-shows-how-romans-invented-the-beef-burger/)

695.

A World War II pigeon named Mary of Exeter survived an assassination attempt by a German warhawk, was shot, hit with shrapnel, and survived a bombing of her loft while delivering messages across the English Channel to France.

Reference: (https://en.wikipedia.org/wiki/Mary_of_Exeter)

696.

Animal Planet made a fake documentary claiming the existence of mermaids. Twice.

Reference: (http://www.businessinsider.com/animal-planets-mermaids-mockumentary-2013-5?op=1)

697.

Thundercats, Silverhawks, Tigersharks and most other Rankin and Bass animated works were created in Japan by a team that came from Toei Animation, creators of Dragon Ball, and would go on to join Studio Ghibli.

Reference: (https://en.wikipedia.org/wiki/Rankin/Bass_Productions#History)

698.

The "Rietbrock Geographical Marker", located in the town of Rietbrock, Wisconsin, is the halfway point between the Equator and the North Pole as well as the Greenwich Meridian and the International Date Line.

Reference: (http://www.wisconsinhistoricalmarkers.com/2013/09/45x90-geographical-marker.html)

699.

After office, President Harry Truman decided that he did not wish to be on any corporate payroll, believing that taking advantage of such financial opportunities would diminish the integrity of the office. He had no personal savings. His only income was his old army pension, which was $113 per month.

Reference: (https://www.nytimes.com/2007/03/02/opinion/02iht-edjacoby.4775315.html)

700.

Professional fans can be paid up to $2000 per sports event to pump up the crowd.

Reference: (https://www.si.com/more-sports/2012/08/22/pro-fan1)

701.

Roald Amundsen, who completed the first Northwest Passage in his used fishing boat, decided to leave his boat and crew in the ice and ski 500 miles to Alaska and back so he could telegraph the news to the world.

Reference:(https://en.wikipedia.org/wiki/Roald_Amundsen#Northwest_Passage_(1903%E2%80%931906))

702.

Anne Frank's older sister, Margot also kept a diary, but no trace of it has ever been found.

Reference: (https://en.wikipedia.org/wiki/Margot_Frank)

703.

At the Revolutionary War Battle of Cowpens, American general Daniel Morgan put his most unreliable soldiers in the front line and gave them permission to run after firing three shots at the enemy.

Reference: (https://www.americanheritage.com/content/america%E2%80%99s-most-imitated-battle)

704.

When researchers from the University of Washington trapped and banded crows for an experiment, they wore caveman masks to hide their identities. They could walk freely in the area without masks, but if they donned the masks again, the crows remembered them as evil and dive-bombed them.

Reference: (https://www.audubon.org/magazine/march-april-2016/meet-bird-brainiacs-american-crow)

705.

OkCupid found women using iPhones averaged twice as many sexual partners as those using android devices.

Reference: (https://theblog.okcupid.com/dont-be-ugly-by-accident-b378f261dea4)

706.

The first car phone was installed in 1910 and became advanced by the 1940s with them being installed in limousines and other commercial vehicles.

Reference: (https://www.techwalla.com/articles/the-history-of-car-phones)

707.

The Vietnam Memorial was designed by a 21 year old architecture student for a class project. She got a B+ despite winning the national competition.

Reference: (http://www.history.com/news/the-21-year-old-college-student-who-designed-the-vietnam-memorial)

708.

Graham crackers, graham bread, and graham flour are inspired by, and named after preacher Sylvester Graham.

Reference: (https://en.wikipedia.org/wiki/Graham_cracker)

709.

Fomitopsis betulina, a fungus exclusive to birch trees, has been used historically to strop razors, mount beetles on, and even medicinally back to the days of Ötzi the iceman.

Reference: (https://en.wikipedia.org/wiki/Fomitopsis_betulina)

710.

Boanthropy is a psychological disorder in which the sufferer believes he or she is a cow or ox. The most famous sufferer of this condition was King Nebuchadnezzar, who in the Book of Daniel, "was driven from men and did eat grass as oxen".

Reference: (https://www.learning-mind.com/10-strangest-psychological-disorders-youve-never-heard-of/)

711.

Benjamin Franklin had written an essay about Flatulence called "Fart Proudly". The essay goes on to discuss methods to essentially make farts not only smell inoffensive but also as agreeable as perfumes.

Reference: (http://allthatsinteresting.com/ben-franklin-fart-proudly)

712.

The United States spent around $100 billion preparing for Y2K.

Reference:(http://www.slate.com/articles/technology/technology/features/2009/apocalypse_then/was_y2k_a_waste.html)

713.

The skull Glenn Danzig used for his logo and the band Samhain came from a comic book called Crystar.

Reference: (http://greenandblackmusic.com/home/2016/08/17/not-of-this-world-the-danzig-skull-and-the-saga-of-crystar/)

714.

NASA hires a chief sniffer to inspect the smell of every item before it enters space. The lack of ventilation means astronauts are stuck with the smells that are onboard with them.

Reference: (https://spaceflight.nasa.gov/shuttle/support/people/galdrich.html)

715.

Tech N9ne put Kendrick Lamar and Jay Rock on to TDE and boosted their rise to fame. Both Kendrick and Jay are featured for their first times namelessly in Tech N9ne's.

Reference: (https://hiphopdx.com/news/id.27452/title.tech-n9ne-says-kendrick-lamar-met-dr-dre-on-his-tour)

716.

Scientists have conducted genome wide association studies to identify the genetic basis of breast size in women.

Reference: (https://www.ncbi.nlm.nih.gov/pmc/articles/PMC3483246/)

717.

In 1868, the USS Wateree was stranded a quarter mile from the ocean after being carried inland by a tsunami. After 9 years of various use as a hospital, inn and warehouse, it was destroyed by another tsunami. Parts of the boilers remain and are now a National Monument of Chile.

Reference: (https://en.wikipedia.org/wiki/USS_Wateree_(1863))

718.

There's a popular burping contest named "Ruttosound" in Italy where burpers are rated for the decibels, singing accuracy, and burp length.

Reference: (https://www.youtube.com/watch?v=REO9kBVxwPI)

719.

The abbreviation "lb" for pound comes from the ancient Roman unit of measure "libra pondo", meaning "a pound by weight", which is also why we ended up calling it a "pound".

Reference: (https://www.britannica.com/science/pound-unit-of-weight)

720.

President Jimmy Carter still gives sermons every other Sunday in his hometown church in Plains, Georgia and is open to the public.

Reference: (http://www.mbcplains.org/?page_id=212)

721.

The river Ombla in Croatia is only 30 meters long and is considered a candidate for the world's shortest river.

Reference:(https://en.wikipedia.org/wiki/Ombla?q=Ombla&_ext=EiQpXWrGmnhWRUAxbRo+lvwiMkA5XWrGmnhWRUBBbRo+lvwiMkA%3D)

722.

The hammer-headed bat is the largest bat in Africa. It has been observed attacking live chickens. With a lifespan of over 30 years, it is also a carrier of the Ebola virus.

Reference: (https://en.wikipedia.org/wiki/Hammer-headed_bat)

723.

Officials in Aliso Viejo tried to ban Dihydrogen Monoxide before finding out it was just water.

Reference: (http://articles.latimes.com/2004/mar/13/local/me-water13)

724.

Fish which can walk out of water and breathe on land for six days could spell major disaster for wildlife in Australia.

Reference: (https://www.independent.co.uk/news/world/australasia/fish-which-walks-out-of-water-and-breathes-on-land-for-six-days-could-spell-major-disaster-for-10295068.html#gallery)

725.

Feng shui practitioners in China find superstitious and corrupt officials easy prey. In one instance, in 2009, county officials in Gansu, on the advice of feng shui practitioners, spent $732,000 to haul a 369-ton "spirit rock" to the county seat to ward off "bad luck."

Reference: (https://en.wikipedia.org/wiki/Feng_shui#Traditional_feng_shui_2)

726.

The President Calvin Coolidge Historic House, where he lived from 1906 to 1930 during the height of his political career, is unusual because he rented rather than owned it. It is also a duplex.

Reference: (https://en.wikipedia.org/wiki/Calvin_Coolidge_House)

727.

Sprinkling granulated sugar on a prolapsed rectum is a certified medical procedure.

Reference: (https://www.aliem.com/2010/09/trick-of-trade-pour-some-sugar-on-me/)

728.

Vietnam is building its first 2 metro systems: one in Hanoi with Chinese funding and the other in Ho Chi Minh City with Japanese expertise. Hanoi's is progressing more quickly but has had multiple accidents, one deadly. HCM City's has had more delays but no accidents.

Reference: (http://www.scmp.com/week-asia/business/article/2104149/vietnams-tale-two-metros-one-built-japanese-and-other-chinese)

729.

A study found that women who had eaten the equivalent of a small packet of crisps a day had double the risk of endometrial cancer and ovarian cancer than women who hadn't.

Reference: (https://www.telegraph.co.uk/news/uknews/1571290/Study-finds-acrylamide-link-to-cancer-in-women.html)

730.

Future's DJ, DJ Esco, was stuck in a Dubai jail for 56 days in 2015.

Reference: (http://www.thefader.com/2015/01/28/dj-esco-spent-56-days-in-dubai-jail-this-is-his-story)

731.

Bellingham, Washington, is the northernmost city with a population of almost 100,000 residents in the contiguous United States.

Reference: (https://en.wikipedia.org/wiki/Bellingham,_Washington)

732.

In 1993, a strange seismic blast occurred in the Australian outback that felt like an earthquake, but many believed it was the work of a Japanese doomsday cult who recruited Soviet scientists and detonated their own nuclear weapon.

Reference: (https://www.nytimes.com/1997/01/21/science/seismic-mystery-in-australia-quake-meteor-or-nuclear-blast.html)

733.

In the past, some young women had all their teeth taken out and replaced by dentures as a 21st birthday present, or as a form of dowry before marriage.

Reference: (https://www.independent.co.uk/news/uk/home-news/smile-a-perfect-smile-but-dont-laugh-we-have-officially-lost-our-dentures-1336158.html)

734.

The number 250 in Mandarin Chinese is an insult meaning stupid person or simpleton.

Reference: (https://en.wikipedia.org/wiki/250_(number))

735.

In 1968, North Korea, stalked, attacked then captured a U.S. naval ship leaving one dead. The ship is currently a museum in Pyongyang.

Reference: (https://en.wikipedia.org/wiki/USS_Pueblo_(AGER-2))

736.

York Factory in Northern Canada was one of the first fur-trading posts established from 1684 and a settlement in Canada. Now operated by Parks Canada, no one lives there aside from a summer residence for staff and nearby seasonal hunting camps.

Reference: (https://en.wikipedia.org/wiki/York_Factory)

737.

The Garfield House Historical Site is one of the most accurately restored and highly detailed of the 19th-century U.S. presidential sites. Of its hundreds of antique Victorian furniture, over 80% was owned by the Garfield family. It also includes the first presidential library.

Reference: (https://en.wikipedia.org/wiki/James_A._Garfield_National_Historic_Site)

738.

Freddie Mercury wrote a love song to his cat.

Reference: (https://www.youtube.com/watch?v=yEYRoXWmWYU)

739.

The Windsor Hum is a deep, rhythmic, droning sound emanating from the secretive U.S. Steel property in Detroit called Zug Island which is causing migraines, nausea, and "revving" vibrations throughout the night.

Reference: (http://www.dailydetroit.com/2017/06/13/video-vice-news-takes-look-mysterious-windsor-hum-zug-island/)

740.

Humpty Dumpty was originally a cannon, which fell off its wall during a siege in the English Civil War.

Reference: (https://www.huffingtonpost.com.au/2017/10/23/why-is-humpty-dumpty-an-egg-an-investigation_a_23253276/)

741.

The People's Republic of Kampuchea was founded by Vietnam and rebuilt Cambodia after the Khmer Rouge, despite being despised by most of the world.

Reference: (https://en.wikipedia.org/wiki/People's_Republic_of_Kampuchea)

742.

Dean Martin had a son named Dean Jr. and a daughter named Deana.

Reference: (https://en.wikipedia.org/wiki/Dean_Martin)

743.

Lucille Ball would send birthday flowers each year to her close friend Carol Burnett. The last delivery arrived on Carol's 56th birthday, hours after Lucy had died.

Reference: (https://en.wikipedia.org/wiki/Lucille_Ball#Later_career)

744.

Alben Barkley married Jane when he was 71 and she was 38. They had both outlived previous spouses. After maintaining a long-distance relationship, they tied the knot and stayed together until he died at 78.

Reference: (https://en.wikipedia.org/wiki/Alben_W._Barkley)

745.

In 1911, 303 Chinese residents were massacred by Mexican rebels in the city of Torreón, Coahuila. The motive was ethnic hatred of the Chinese.

Reference: (https://en.wikipedia.org/wiki/Torre%C3%B3n_massacre)

746.

One of Leo Tolstoy's many short stories was lauded as the, "greatest story that the literature of the world knows", by James Joyce in a letter to his daughter.

Reference: (https://en.wikipedia.org/wiki/How_Much_Land_Does_a_Man_Need%3F)

747.

One can obtain a driver's license as young as 14.5 years in South Dakota.

Reference: (https://www.verywellfamily.com/driving-age-by-state-2611172)

748.

Plants can develop abnormally causing leafy structures to develop instead of blossoms.

Reference: (https://en.wikipedia.org/wiki/Phyllody)

749.

The United States Navy has a combat dolphin program.

Reference: (https://en.wikipedia.org/wiki/Military_dolphin#United_States_Navy_dolphins)

750.

American Civil War Union soldiers were issued 36 pounds of coffee a year and the word "coffee" appeared more in journal entries than "war," "bullet," "cannon," "slavery," "mother" or "Lincoln."

Reference: (https://www.npr.org/sections/thesalt/2016/07/25/485227943/if-war-is-hell-then-coffee-has-offered-u-s-soldiers-some-salvation)

751.

Sokushinbutsu is the Buddhist practice of observing asceticism to the point of death and mummification while alive. Only 24 monks have been discovered achieving this.

Reference: (https://io9.gizmodo.com/the-gruesome-and-excruciating-practice-of-mummifying-yo-1515905564)

752.

Abraham Lincoln ran for state legislature in 1834 in part because he needed a well-paying job to pay off his debt.

Reference:(https://en.wikipedia.org/wiki/Early_life_and_career_of_Abraham_Lincoln#Politics_and_the_law)

753.

In 2017, three infertile mice were able to give birth to healthy offspring after being implanted with artificial 3-D printed ovaries.

Reference: (https://www.smithsonianmag.com/smart-news/functional-3d-printed-ovary-transplanted-mice-180963337/)

754.

The mathematical field Algebra is named after the book "Al-jabr" by Islamic mathematician Muhammad ibn Musa al-Khwarizmi.

Reference: (https://en.wikipedia.org/wiki/History_of_algebra#Islamic_algebra)

755.

Small framed 120 pound Molly Schuyler smashed the world record on April 19th, 2015, by eating three 72 ounce steaks, 3 shrimp cocktails, 3 baked potatoes, 3 salads and 3 bread rolls in 20 minutes. The "Texas King" is free to anyone than can eat it in an hour or less at The Big Texan, Amarillo.

Reference: (https://en.wikipedia.org/wiki/The_Big_Texan_Steak_Ranch)

756.

Stephen King considers "Dolores Umbridge" from Harry Potter and The Order of the Phoenix the, "Greatest made up villain since Hannibal Lecter."

Reference: (http://ew.com/books/2009/08/01/harry-potter-and-order-phoenix-4/)

757.

Everest climber Lincoln Hall was presumed dead and abandoned at 8700 meters. The next morning, a group of climbers found him changing his clothes, alive, awake, and almost naked.

Reference: (https://en.wikipedia.org/wiki/Lincoln_Hall_(climber))

758.

The inflatable tube man was invented by Trinidad and Tobago artist Peter Minshall for the 1996 Summer Olympics. Minshall originally called it "Tall Boy".

Reference: (https://en.wikipedia.org/wiki/Tube_man)

759.

Jimmy Carter was considered such a long shot candidate that when he told his mother, Lillian, his plans to run for President, she asked him "President of what?"

Reference: (https://www.khanacademy.org/humanities/ap-us-history/period-8/apush-the-1970s/a/the-presidency-of-jimmy-carter)

760.

Keith Richards, guitarist and founding member of the Rolling Stones, has been quoted as saying that he yearns to be a librarian.

Reference: (https://en.wikipedia.org/wiki/Keith_Richards#Public_image_and_private_life)

761.

Before humans traveled to space, many monkeys were launched into space so that scientists could study their biological response to space travel.

Reference: (https://en.wikipedia.org/wiki/Monkeys_and_apes_in_space)

762.

Archer doesn't have a team of writers; the only writer is the creator, Adam Reed.

Reference: (https://en.wikipedia.org/wiki/Archer_(TV_series)#Writing)

763.

There was a floating McDonalds called the "McBarge."

Reference: (https://www.youtube.com/watch?v=W9mc4PsXU5E&t=607s)

764.

BMI is a terrible measure of individual health because it was never even intended to measure individual health but to give a quick and easy way to measure the degree of obesity of the general population.

Reference: (https://www.npr.org/templates/story/story.php?storyId=106268439)

765.

About 25% of people with tattoos regret the decision, averaging to about 7.5 million Americans.

Reference: (https://www.medicaldaily.com/g00/tattoos-affect-your-health-long-term-side-effects-ink-has-your-immune-system-404404?i10c.encReferrer=aHR0cHM6Ly93d3cucmVkZGl0LmNvbS9yL3RvZGF5aWxlYXJuZWQvbmV3Lz9jb3VudD03NTAmYWZ0ZXI9dDNfOGpxbzJy&i10c.ua=1&i10c.dv=14)

766.

Julia Popova was stabbed by a mugger as she walked home from work in 2010, but she was so traumatized by the attack that she walked home without realizing the knife was embedded in her, just a fraction of an inch from her spinal cord.

Reference: (http://www.globaltimes.cn/content/503913.shtml)

767.

In 1494, Pope Alexander VI decreed that any land inhabited by non-Christians could be colonized by Europeans on the basis of "discovery". In 1823, this decree by the Pope was upheld by the U.S. Supreme Court in the Johnson v. M'Intosh case, setting a legal precedent for Manifest Destiny.

Reference: (https://www.gilderlehrman.org/sites/default/files/inline-pdfs/04093_FPS.pdf)

768.

In 2018, China banned actors with tattoos and hip-hop culture from television.

Reference: (http://time.com/5112061/china-hip-hop-ban-tattoos-television/)

769.

In 1972, Nixon's senior staff plotted to kill journalist Jack Anderson by poisoning him or staging a fatal mugging.

Reference: (https://en.wikipedia.org/wiki/Jack_Anderson_(columnist))

770.

In 2010, Campbell's "25% less sodium" tomato soup had the same amount of sodium as their "regular" tomato soup, with both containing 480 milligrams.

Reference: (https://consumerist.com/2011/04/18/campbells-soup-sued-over-sodium-claims/)

771.

Henriette von Schirach, the daughter of Hitler's personal photographer, once publicly confronted the dictator about the mistreatment of Jews. Hitler got deeply hurt and soon left the room.

Reference: (https://en.wikipedia.org/wiki/Henriette_von_Schirach)

772.

"Motherfucker" is Samuel L. Jackson's favorite affirmation to help overcome his stutter.

Reference: (https://en.wikipedia.org/wiki/Samuel_L._Jackson?repost)

773.

Rob Knox, who played Marcus Belby in "Harry Potter and the Half Blood Prince" was stabbed to death outside a bar in London while protecting his younger brother from two men, one of whom was armed with two knives. He was 18.

Reference: (https://en.wikipedia.org/wiki/Rob_Knox)

774.

Josh Brolin's stepmother is Barbra Streisand.

Reference: (https://en.wikipedia.org/wiki/Josh_Brolin)

775.

The divide between night and day on Earth is called the Terminator.

Reference: (https://www.universetoday.com/73622/terminator/)

776.

The word "Halitosis" was created as an ad campaign to sell Listerine, originally invented as a surgical antiseptic, as a mouthwash.

Reference: (https://www.smithsonianmag.com/smart-news/marketing-campaign-invented-halitosis-180954082/)

777.

There are only 3 countries where the majority has a favorable view of Russia: Greece (64%), Philippines (55%) and Vietnam (83%).

Reference: (http://www.pewglobal.org/2017/08/16/publics-worldwide-unfavorable-toward-putin-russia/)

778.

Bubble wrap was invented accidentally after failed attempts to create plastic, 3-D wallpaper.

Reference: (https://en.wikipedia.org/wiki/Bubble_wrap)

779.

The City Wall of Nanjing was among the largest city walls ever constructed in China. It took 21 years to complete, used 200,000 laborers to move 7 million cubic meters of earth and was also the longest city wall in the world until the 17th century.

Reference: (https://en.wikipedia.org/wiki/City_Wall_of_Nanjing)

780.

Zimbabwe's bank balance was a total of just $217 at the start of 2013.

Reference: (http://www.bbc.com/news/world-africa-21257765)

781.

Teddy Roosevelt and his son killed 512 animals on a safari in 1909. The menagerie includes: 17 lions, 29 zebras, 27 gazelles, 9 black and white monkeys, 8 hippopotami, 2 ostriches, a pelican, and 4 crocodiles.

Reference: (https://www.vox.com/2015/7/29/9067587/theodore-roosevelt-safari)

782.

Shell Oil got its start in 1833 when an antiques dealer started importing shells from the Far East for interior design.

Reference: (https://www.shell.com/about-us/who-we-are/our-beginnings.html#vanity-aHR0cHM6Ly93d3cuc2hlbGwuY29tL2dsb2JhbC9hYm91dHNoZWxsL3dob13ZS1hcmUvb3VyLWhpc3RvcnkvdGhlLWJlZ2lubmluZ3MuaHRtbA)

783.

Vancouver's Beaty Biodiversity Museum has a 25-metre skeleton of a female blue whale suspended over the ramp leading to the main collections, making it the largest skeleton exhibit in the world suspended without external framework for support.

Reference: (https://en.wikipedia.org/wiki/Beaty_Biodiversity_Museum)

784.

In 1944, by a huge coincidence, a crossword puzzle was printed with answers all containing D-Day operation "code names", which sent MI-5 into a panic thinking their invasion plans had been discovered.

Reference: (https://www.historic-uk.com/HistoryUK/HistoryofBritain/Crossword-Panic-of-1944/)

785.

Wendy's chocolate Frosty is actually half chocolate and half vanilla because owner Dave Thomas thought full chocolate would be too overpowering a flavor paired with their burger and fries meal.

Reference: (https://en.wikipedia.org/wiki/Frosty_(frozen_dairy_dessert))

786.

In 1987, a Kentucky teacher was fired for showing the movie "Pink Floyd: The Wall", after her students voted to watch it. She appealed the firing all the way to the Supreme Court. During the appeal process, 6th circuit court Judge H. Ted Milburn called the film "gross and bizarre".

Reference: (http://ultimateclassicrock.com/pink-floyd-the-wall-movie-teacher/)

787.

The voice you hear in your head while reading is known as subvocalization.

Reference: (https://en.wikipedia.org/wiki/Subvocalization)

788.

Despite its name, Frank Sinatra's song "My Way" was written by others. It was originally a French song called "Comme d'habitude", which was rewritten for Sinatra by none other than Paul Anka himself.

Reference: (https://en.wikipedia.org/wiki/My_Way)

789.

Air Nauru's Boeing 737-300 consumed nearly 30% of the nation's GDP and the near-bankrupt airline was seized by creditors in Australia which left the nation without any air service in 2005.

Reference: (https://en.wikipedia.org/wiki/Nauru_International_Airport)

790.

In 2011, a 75 year old Georgian woman accidentally cut off internet access to almost all of Armenia while scavenging for copper to sell as scrap.

Reference: (https://www.theguardian.com/world/2011/apr/06/georgian-woman-cuts-web-access)

791.

In 1949, Montreal and Toronto experienced large spikes in the use of $2 banknotes for financial transactions. As the spike subsided over two weeks, another one appeared in Ottawa. The Bank of Canada could provide no explanation.

Reference: (https://en.wikipedia.org/wiki/1937_Series_(banknotes))

792.

SOS messages have been found stitched in Primark clothing, allegedly from employees complaining of "sweatshop conditions" and being "worked like oxen" over 15 hour shifts.

Reference: (https://en.wikipedia.org/wiki/Primark#SOS_Messages)

793.

In 2015, some Instagram filter names rose in popularity as actual names. One in particular, Lux, rose 75% in popularity. Other names include Ludwig, Amaro, Reyes, Hudson, Kelvin, Juno, Valencia, and Willow.

Reference: (http://time.com/4130646/baby-names-instagram-2015/)

794.

The longest confirmed family tree records belong to Chinese philosopher Confucius, stretching over 2500 years and an estimated 3 million descendants.

Reference: (https://people.howstuffworks.com/culture-traditions/genealogy/longest-existing-family-tree.htm)

795.

Boxers Jack Johnson and Joe Choynski were arrested in Texas, because while boxing exhibitions were legal, prize fighting was not. While the two were in jail, the sheriff allowed crowds to gather to watch the two men spar.

Reference: (http://boxrec.com/media/index.php/Joe_Choynski_vs._Jack_Johnson)

796.

In the original Swedish version of "Survivor", the first person to be voted out of the first season committed suicide a month later.

Reference: (https://en.wikipedia.org/wiki/Expedition_Robinson_1997)

797.

When Tintin comics were first published in the U.S. in the 1950's, all panels depicting "free mixing of the races" were censored or removed altogether.

Reference: (https://en.wikipedia.org/wiki/The_Adventures_of_Tintin#American)

798.

Werner Herzog once promised fellow documentary maker Errol Morris that he would eat his shoe if Morris ever finished his movie on pet cemeteries, because he found Morris to be incapable of ever finishing his projects. In 1978, Morris finished his film, and Herzog publicly cooked and ate his shoe.

Reference: (https://en.wikipedia.org/wiki/Werner_Herzog#Career)

799.

Elvis Presley was a natural blonde. He dyed his hair black for an edgier look.

Reference: (http://www.thesundayleader.lk/2011/12/25/ten-things-you-didnt-know-about-elvis-presley/)

800.

There is a speed camera lottery in Stockholm, Sweden. Drive at or under the speed limit and you'll be entered into a lottery where the prize fund comes from the fines that speeders pay.

Reference: (https://www.wired.com/2010/12/swedish-speed-camera-pays-drivers-to-slow-down/)

801.

Edward Bernays the nephew of Sigmund Freud, who was nicknamed "the father of public relations", created a campaign in 1929 to promote female smoking by branding cigarettes as feminist "Torches of Freedom".

Reference: (https://en.wikipedia.org/wiki/Edward_Bernays)

802.

The Looney Tunes skunk character Pepe Le Pew was inspired by Mel Blanc's "ladies man" colleague at Termite Terrace, Tedd Pierce. However, the name came from Charles Boyer's character Pepe Le Moko in Algiers, and Blanc used a character voice he had created for Jack Benny's radio show.

Reference: (https://en.wikipedia.org/wiki/Pep%C3%A9_Le_Pew#Production)

803.

Ethiopian multiplication is a method of multiplication that involves repeatedly halving one number and doubling the other one and using that to multiply the original two numbers.

Reference: (https://rosettacode.org/wiki/Ethiopian_multiplication)

804.

Mr. Rogers once convinced the Senate to fund PBS instead of the Vietnam War.

Reference: (https://www.themarysue.com/drunk-history-mister-rogers/#utm_source=reddit&utm_medium=TIL&utm_campaign=shares)

805.

Commercial pilots sound the same because they're all basing their voice on Chuck Yeager's.

Reference: (https://www.techly.com.au/2015/09/16/familiar-pattern-commerical-pilots-voices-can-traced-back-one-american-fighter-pilot/)

806.

A plan by Germany was made to capture France through Belgium, but Belgium had a treaty with Britain which meant Britain would come to the aid of Belgium and Britain declared a war on Germany which extended for 4 years and killed 1.8 million German soldiers. Now, we call that World War I.

Reference: (https://en.wikipedia.org/wiki/Schlieffen_Plan)

807.

Over a five-year period starting in 1968, commercial jets were hijacked nearly once a week in the United States.

Reference: (https://theskiesbelongtous.com/the-story/)

808.

The asteroid belt has a dwarf planet within it which also has mysterious ice volcanos.

Reference: (https://en.wikipedia.org/wiki/Ceres_(dwarf_planet))

809.

The celebrity tabloid TMZ stands for Thirty Mile Zone, an invisible circle with a radius of 30 miles that was negotiated by unions to be considered local. Filming outside this circle is very expensive because then cast and crew need to be compensated for their commute.

Reference: (https://www.youtube.com/watch?v=yy16KFzM4XU)

810.

Josephine Baker, the glamorous Jazz-age singer and dancer, was recruited by the Deuxième Bureau, the French intelligence service, initially to report on what she heard and observed with her unique access, and later to communicate internationally via invisible ink on the back of her sheet music.

Reference: (https://www.thedailybeast.com/when-jazz-age-superstar-josephine-baker-spied-on-the-nazis)

811.

Even though they were being constantly shelled and bombed, the British forces waiting to be evacuated from Dunkirk would queue up patiently for hours.

Reference: (https://www.theguardian.com/world/2017/jul/16/dunkirk-darkest-day-29-may-1940-evacuation-came-close-to-disaster)

812.

Water itself isn't wet. It makes other solid materials wet.

Reference: (http://scienceline.ucsb.edu/getkey.php?key=6097)

813.

McMurdo Station in Antarctica had a nuclear reactor from 1964 to 1972 that had over 438 malfunctions, 223 reports of abnormal levels of radiation were recorded and leaked dangerous radiation.

Reference: (http://large.stanford.edu/courses/2014/ph241/reid2/)

814.

The Civil Rights Act of 1964 was passed after an 83-day filibuster ended. The day before, a hotel owner in St. Augustine, Florida had dumped acid into his swimming pool that white and black bathers sought to integrate. The protesters were then arrested.

Reference: (https://www.npr.org/2014/06/13/321380585/remembering-a-civil-rights-swim-in-it-was-a-milestone)

815.

The power of potatoes, voltage wise, can be stronger than electric eels.

Reference: (http://www.guinnessworldrecords.com/world-records/highest-voltage-from-a-potato-battery/)

816.

In August 2010, a massive traffic jam started in Beijing and continued for more than 100 kilometers, or 62 miles, into Inner Mongolia, lasting for two weeks.

Reference: (https://en.wikipedia.org/wiki/China_National_Highway_110_traffic_jam)

817.

Tuataras are lizard-like reptiles, though not lizards, endemic to New Zealand. They are extremely long-lived, with successful breeding between a 110 year old male and 80 year old female.

Reference: (https://en.wikipedia.org/wiki/Tuatara#Reproduction)

818.

The actual name for a Chinese takeout box is an Oyster Pail. They were originally used to carry opened oysters so the customer didn't have to shuck them, and were re-purposed after the over-fishing of oysters in the mid-20th century.

Reference: (https://en.wikipedia.org/wiki/Oyster_pail)

819.

The snow on the poppy field in the "Wizard of Oz" was 100% asbestos.

Reference: (https://www.asbestos.net/asbestos/products/fake-snow/)

820.

Adam Sandler actually pelted those children with dodgeballs in Billy Madison. He ended up making one of the kids cry. The parents were not happy and approached Sandler. He responded and said, "Didn't they read the script?" and the parent said "They're six, they don't read yet."

Reference: (http://ew.com/tv/2017/03/16/adam-sandler-made-child-actor-cry-bill-madison-conan/)

821.

Alan Arbus, who played psychiatrist Dr. Sidney Freedman on "M*A*S*H," was married to photographer Diane Arbus, who committed suicide.

Reference: (https://www.nytimes.com/2013/04/24/arts/television/allan-arbus-mash-actor-dies-at-95.html)

822.

Because JVC licensed VHS to any manufacturer, they won the videotape format war over Sony's Betamax.

Reference: (https://en.wikipedia.org/wiki/Videotape_format_war#Outcome)

823.

There is a whiskey made from the urine of elderly diabetics.

Reference: (http://jamesgilpin.com/gilpin-family-whisky/)

824.

An organ in Germany is currently playing a composition by John Cage called "As Slow As Possible." The piece will take 639 years to complete. The most recent note change was in 2013, the next will be in 2020.

Reference: (https://en.wikipedia.org/wiki/As_Slow_as_Possible)

825.

It takes 1,000,000 liters of diesel to fill the fuel tank on the president of United Arab Emirates yacht.

Reference: (http://www.yachting-pages.com/content/how-much-fuel-does-it-take-to-fill-a-superyacht-guide.html)

826.

On the set of "Hatari!" shot in Africa, John Wayne and co-star Red Buttons were playing cards outside when a leopard come out of the bush towards them. When Buttons mentioned the approaching leopard, Wayne said, "See what he wants."

Reference: (https://en.wikipedia.org/wiki/Hatari!#Production)

827.

On their 2000 album "Hooray for Boobies", the Bloodhound Gang included a track called "The Ten Coolest Things About New Jersey". The song is just ten seconds of silence.

Reference: (https://en.wikipedia.org/wiki/Hooray_for_Boobies#Style)

828.

After the Battle of Shiloh in 1862, during the Civil War, soldiers reported a peculiar phenomenon: glow-in-the-dark wounds later called "Angel Glow."

Reference: (http://www.americancivilwarstory.com/angels-glow-shiloh.html)

829.

The word "robot" comes from a Czech word meaning "forced labor."

Reference: (https://www.sciencefriday.com/segments/science-diction-the-origin-of-the-word-robot/)

830.

Michael Jackson made a Pepsi commercial using Billie Jean.

Reference: (https://www.youtube.com/watch?v=MMkV2Vi0MKA)

831.

In 2011, several remarkably expensive bowls of pho were auctioned off for charity. AnQi Phở was prepared with type A5-Wagyu beef, white truffles, precious foie gras broth, and perfectly manicured noodles made of rare blue lobster meat.

Reference: (https://en.wikipedia.org/wiki/Pho)

832.

"Burped" speech can act as an alternative means of vocalization for people who have undergone a laryngectomy, the removal of the larynx, with the burp replacing laryngeal phonation.

Reference: (https://en.wikipedia.org/wiki/Burping#%22Burped%22_speech)

833.

German pharmaceutical company Bayer originally manufactured heroin in 1898 as a treatment for morphine addiction.

Reference: (https://www.drugfreeworld.org/drugfacts/heroin.html)

834.

In the U.K., the common man and wealthy women received the right to vote only 10 years before the common woman and included allowing women to run for MP.

Reference: (https://en.wikipedia.org/wiki/Women%27s_suffrage_in_the_United_Kingdom)

835.

In 1993, Michael Jackson patented a shoe that allowed him to do the Smooth Criminal lean during live shows without using wires.

Reference: (https://mashable.com/2015/03/28/michael-jackson-shoe-patent/#qoVPr9MXSmqn)

836.

Pilots named the F-16 fighter jet "Viper" after the Colonial Viper in 1970's "Battlestar Galactica."

Reference: (https://en.wikipedia.org/wiki/Colonial_Viper)

837.

The Hulk was originally intended to be grey and became green due to a printing press malfunction.

Reference: (http://resources.willowprint.com/willow/index.asp?jx=fv_49)

838.

Cicadas use organs called tymbals to produce a unique mating call as loud as 120 decibels, near the pain threshold of the human ear. Scientists still don't fully understand how tymbals produce sound at such a high volume.

Reference: (https://animals.howstuffworks.com/insects/question733.htm)

839.

Adele's "Someone Like You" was co-written by Dan Wilson, who also wrote Semisonic's "Closing Time".

Reference: (http://variety.com/2017/music/news/adele-songwriter-semisonic-dan-wilson-album-re-covered-1202509330/)

840.

After one of the bloodiest mutinies in history, a British frigate was delivered to the Spanish. Viewing it a matter of honor, Captain Hamilton of the HMS Surprise took 100 men into a heavily fortified harbor and retook the ship, killing or capturing 350 Spanish without losing any of his own.

Reference: (https://en.wikipedia.org/wiki/Cutting_out_of_the_Hermione)

841.

SOS doesn't really stand for anything. In fact, the signal isn't even really supposed to be three individual letters. It's just a continuous Morse code string of three dots, three dashes, and three dots all run together with no spaces or full stops (...---...).

Reference: (http://mentalfloss.com/article/31911/what-does-sos-stand)

842.

A woman refused to board a lifeboat when the Titanic was sinking as she refused to be parted from her dog. Several days later, passengers on the SS Bremen passing by the wreckage in the water, saw the body of a woman tightly holding a large shaggy dog in her arms.

Reference: (https://en.wikipedia.org/wiki/Animals_aboard_the_RMS_Titanic)

843.

Stephen King kept a severe alcohol and cocaine addiction hidden from his family for eight years. He claims he kept the addiction well-hidden but eventually, "...the books [started] to show it after a while. 'Misery' is a book about cocaine. Annie Wilkes is cocaine. She was my number-one fan."

Reference: (https://en.wikipedia.org/wiki/Misery_(novel)#Background)

844.

Most foods are safely consumable 2 to 3 years past their expiration date as the FDA has no regulation of these numbers. It's estimated that 40% of all the annual food waste in the USA is able to be healthily consumed.

Reference: (https://www.foodindustry.com/articles/how-food-expiration-dates-contribute-food-waste/)

845.

Before the Acts of Union in 1707, where Scotland formed a Union with England, the "Scottish Empire" comprised of colonies in the Americas.

Reference: (https://en.wikipedia.org/wiki/Scottish_colonization_of_the_Americas)

846.

American beer is generally bland because 19th-century brewers were trying to convince Prohibition supporters that beer was a healthier and cleaner drink than whiskey and other liquors.

Reference: (http://host.madison.com/lifestyles/food-and-cooking/why-bland-american-beer-is-here-to-stay/article_7f5e9db2-36fd-52ab-9c6c-543c3e5d16b0.html)

847.

The cost of raising a child in the U.S. has increased considerably over the years to $233,610 with housing accounting for 29% of the cost with some kids costing close to $400,000 averages.

Reference: (http://time.com/money/4629700/child-raising-cost-department-of-agriculture-report/)

848.

Platypuses don't have nipples. Despite being mammals and having mammary glands, platypuses do not have nipples with which to feed their babies. Instead, they release milk through glands like sweat. The milk then gathers in grooves on the mum's abdomen where the puggles lap it up.

Reference: (http://ipfactly.com/platypus-facts-for-kids-questions-answered/)

849.

Nicholas II, the Last Tsar of the Russian Empire, had a black dragon tattoo on his forearm. During his stay in a Nagasaki harbor on a Russian battleship, he asked to be introduced to artists, so the next day an artist came and tattooed his right forearm with a black dragon.

Reference: (https://www.slavorum.org/nicholas-ii-the-tsar-with-the-dragon-tattoo/)

850.

Starbucks followed McDonald's to offer free Wi-Fi, not the other way around. McDonald's started offering free Wi-Fi in some countries in 2007 and earlier, and throughout the USA in January 2010. Starbucks didn't start with free Wi-Fi until July 2010.

Reference: (https://www.cbsnews.com/news/mcdonalds-to-offer-free-wifi/)

851.

Jesus cursed a fig tree because it wouldn't give him fruit.

Reference: (https://www.biblegateway.com/passage/?search=Matthew+21%3A18-22&version=NIV)

852.

At the coronation of Elizabeth I in January 1559, a dozen or so cats were stuffed into a wickerwork effigy of the Pope and paraded through the streets of London before being burned on a bonfire. Their dying shrieks were said to be of the devils inhabiting the Pope's body.

Reference: (https://www.theanneboleynfiles.com/tudor-cats/)

853.

Martin Amis wrote an entire book about playing Space Invaders.

Reference: (https://themillions.com/2012/02/the-arcades-project-martin-amis-guide-to-classic-video-games.html)

854.

The traditional Japanese color Namakabe-iro translates to English as "The color of an undried wall".

Reference: (https://en.wikipedia.org/wiki/Traditional_colors_of_Japan)

855.

"Tarzan" actor Johnny Weissmuller was playing golf during the Cuban Revolution when his cart was suddenly surrounded by rebel soldiers. After doing the Tarzan yell for them, the guerrillas recognized him and even escorted him to his hotel.

Reference: (https://en.wikipedia.org/wiki/Johnny_Weissmuller#After_films)

856.

L. Ron Hubbard has more fiction published than anyone who has ever lived.

Reference: (http://wikipedia.org/wiki/Written_works_of_L._Ron_Hubbard)

857.

Ted Turner, creator of TNT, Cartoon Network, TBS, and CNN, managed one Atlanta Braves game in 1977. He was the owner of the team at the time and after the Braves lost 16 straight games he told the manager of the team to take a break and Turner then took over for the game after.

Reference: (http://www.espn.com/blog/playbook/fandom/post/_/id/22066/the-night-ted-turner-managed-the-braves)

858.

S.M. was known as the woman with no fear. Scientists tested her by having her handle snakes and spiders, watch scary movies, and go through a haunted house.

Reference: (https://en.wikipedia.org/wiki/S.M._(patient))

859.

When you stop smoking weed, you're going to experience a huge increase in your dreams and their vividness due to your brain trying to catch up on all the missed REM sleep for the next 2 to 7 weeks.

Reference: (https://www.leafscience.com/2014/09/13/marijuana-rem-sleep-dreams/)

860.

The Beatles were asked to cameo in the 1965 Doctor Who episode "The Chase" playing older versions of themselves. Their manager, Brian Epstein, said no.

Reference: (http://tardis.wikia.com/wiki/The_Beatles)

861.

In the U.K., sale or charter of Airships is explicitly VAT exempt.

Reference: (https://www.gov.uk/government/publications/vat-notice-744c-ships-aircraft-and-associated-services/vat-notice-744c-ships-aircraft-and-associated-services#aircraft-and-qualifying-aircraft)

862.

Manfred Rommel, son of Field Marshal Erwin Rommel, became the mayor of Stuttgart in 1974, earning various domestic and foreign honors including the German Great Cross of Merit, the U.S. Presidential Medal of Freedom, the British CBE, and the French Legion of Honor throughout his lifetime.

Reference: (https://en.wikipedia.org/wiki/Manfred_Rommel)

863.

Gold farming in China is more pervasive than in any other country, as 80% of all gold farmers are in mainland China, with a total of 100,000 full-time gold farmers in the country as of 2005.

Reference: (https://en.wikipedia.org/wiki/Gold_farming#China)

864.

Harold Holt, the Prime Minister of Australia, who disappeared while swimming and was eventually declared dead, has had two swimming pools named after him.

Reference: (https://en.wikipedia.org/wiki/Disappearance_of_Harold_Holt)

865.

Peace Arch State Park was built on the International Boundary between Canada and the United States to commemorate the lasting peace between the two countries. The southern half of the park is owned by Washington State Parks and the northern half, by British Columbia Provincial Parks.

Reference: (http://www.env.gov.bc.ca/bcparks/explore/parkpgs/peace_arch/)

866.

The dinosaur species Zuul crurivastator was named after the demon and demi-god Zuul, the Gatekeeper of Gozer, featured in the 1984 film "Ghostbusters." This was due to Zuul's head resembling that of an ankylosaur.

Reference: (https://en.wikipedia.org/wiki/Zuul)

867.

Mir Sultan Khan was a servant who was the greatest natural chess player of modern times. In his brief stay in Europe, he defeated former world champion Casablanca before returning to India with his master.

Reference: (https://en.wikipedia.org/wiki/Mir_Sultan_Khan)

868.

The lump in your throat feeling, otherwise known as "globus hystericus," is actually something called a Cricopharyngeal spasm. It is extremely rare for it to indicate a serious condition, and the only known physiological cause is anxiety.

Reference: (https://en.wikipedia.org/wiki/Cricopharyngeal_spasm)

869.

When the Channel Tunnel was built, the British used the excavated chalk to create a little bit of artificial land which is now a park.

Reference: (https://en.wikipedia.org/wiki/Samphire_Hoe_Country_Park)

870.

Italy's first serial killer killed only people who were making love in cars.

Reference: (https://www.youtube.com/watch?v=L2B6oxV-E5g&feature=youtu.be)

871.

Tomatoes and potatoes come from the same family and can be grafted onto each other. This same family includes peppers, eggplants, and strangely enough; tobacco.

Reference: (https://en.wikipedia.org/wiki/Solanaceae)

872.

West and East Berlin used two different kinds of street lights during the Cold War, producing different colors that are still visible from space, almost 30 years after the wall fell.

Reference: (https://www.citymetric.com/horizons/you-can-see-berlin-s-east-west-divide-space-886)

873.

Abraham Lincoln had clinical depression.

Reference: (https://www.theatlantic.com/magazine/archive/2005/10/lincolns-great-depression/304247/)

874.

In the Civil War, confederate general A.P. Hill was often disabled due to the multiple STDs he contracted while in college.

Reference: (https://en.wikipedia.org/wiki/A._P._Hill)

875.

We are 3 times more likely to die from cancer than we were 100 years ago. But we were 10 times more likely to die from the flu back then.

Reference: (https://www.nejm.org/doi/full/10.1056/NEJMp1113569)

876.

In 1973, Icelanders successfully stopped a lava flow that threatened their town by spraying it with seawater.

Reference: (https://en.wikipedia.org/wiki/Eldfell#lava-cooling%20operations)

877.

Gene Wilder did not tell the public about his Alzheimer's diagnosis, because, "He simply couldn't bear the idea of one less smile in the world."

Reference:(http://www.slate.com/blogs/browbeat/2016/08/30/gene_wilder_s_family_issues_a_st atement_on_his_alzheimer_s_and_circumstances.html)

878.

There is a snake, "Boomslang", whose bite can cause people to bleed from every orifice in their body, can cause internal bleeding and will bleed them out for 5 days before they die.

Reference: (https://en.wikipedia.org/wiki/Boomslang)

879.

The first monarch to travel in a submarine was King James I of England in 1620, who had Dutch inventor Cornelis Drebbel construct one in London. Though he only submerged in a test dive, the vessel could travel a few kilometers and stay submerged for three hours.

Reference: (https://en.wikipedia.org/wiki/Cornelis_Drebbel#Submarine)

880.

Microsoft gave the domain Bob.com to a man named Bob in exchange for Windows2000.com

Reference:(https://www.theregister.co.uk/1999/11/11/windows2000_com_owner_sells_domain/)

881.

The top 100 mountain peaks in the world are all in Asia. 99 out of them pass through at least one of India, Nepal, China, Pakistan or Bhutan.

Reference: (https://en.wikipedia.org/wiki/List_of_highest_mountains_on_Earth#By_country)

882.

The oldest plant to be regenerated was grown from 32,000 year old seeds. Russian scientists discovered a seed cache of a native Siberian flowering plant that had been buried by an Ice Age squirrel near a river bank. The seeds, encased in ice, were unearthed from 124 feet below the permafrost.

Reference: (https://news.nationalgeographic.com/news/2012/02/120221-oldest-seeds-regenerated-plants-science/)

883.

There is an asteroid orbiting Jupiter in retrograde, which is the "wrong" direction. Some believe that the asteroid is not native to our Solar System.

Reference: (https://en.wikipedia.org/wiki/(514107)_2015_BZ509)

884.

John Williams' piece "Duel of the Fates" is based on a Celtic poem called "Cad Goddeu," but sung in Sanskrit.

Reference: (https://en.wikipedia.org/wiki/Cad_Goddeu#Other_uses)

885.

"Chicken Shit Bingo" is a weekly event at the Little Longhorn Saloon in Austin, Texas. Participants purchase a ticket which corresponds to a random number on the table. If the chicken defecates on your number you win a cash prize.

Reference: (https://do512.com/p/chicken-shit-bingo)

886.

The song "YYZ" by Rush was named after the Toronto Pearson International Airport in Canada, whose airport identifier code is YYZ. The intro of the song is YYZ in Morse code which can be heard by pilots flying towards the airport.

Reference: (http://www.songfacts.com/detail.php?id=3104)

887.

The explorer Hamilton Hume developed three fine Mariano wool properties while living at the Cooma Cottage in the 1800's.

Reference: (https://findcountryhomes.com/famous-country-homes-around-the-world/)

888.

Magnetic resonance imaging of meat pies is not a reliable method of determining if it contains meat.

Reference: (https://onlinelibrary.wiley.com/doi/full/10.1111/1754-9485.12740)

889.

Richard Jenkins, the actor who played John C. Reilly's father in "Step Brothers" used to drive a linen truck for a living. His boss was John Reilly, John C. Reilly's real-life father.

Reference: (https://www.npr.org/templates/transcript/transcript.php?storyId=100674398)

890.

A secret society called Cicada 3301 has on six occasions posted puzzles and alternate reality games, some lasting years, in an attempt to recruit code breakers from the public.

Reference: (https://en.wikipedia.org/wiki/Cicada_3301)

891.

Both Los Angeles and New York, plus 10 other states, have a city named Long Beach.

Reference: (http://www.funtrivia.com/askft/Question131764.html)

892.

The Boston Celtics have the only NBA court made out of red oak wood. All of the others are made of maple.

Reference: (https://www.si.com/nba/2015/12/02/nba-hardwood-floors-basketball-court-celtics-nets-magic-nuggets-hornets)

893.

Exxon stations are "Esso" stations outside of the United States.

Reference: (https://en.wikipedia.org/wiki/Esso)

894.

Happy hours that discount alcohol are prohibited in Utah.

Reference: (https://sbi.utah.gov/alcohol-enforcement-team/frequently-asked-questions/#happy%20hour)

895.

Nongqawuse was a Xhosa prophet who convinced her people to kill their cattle and destroy their crops, resulting in a famine that killed three quarters of their population.

Reference: (https://en.wikipedia.org/wiki/Nongqawuse)

896.

The 1938 Yellow River flood was a man-made flood caused by the Nationalist Government of China in a failed attempt to stop the Japanese in the early part of the 2nd Sino-Japanese War. It killed an estimated 500,000 people, and shifted the mouth of the river several hundred kilometers south.

Reference: (https://en.wikipedia.org/wiki/1938_Yellow_River_flood)

897.

In the 17th century, choir boys as young as eight years old would be castrated in order to preserve their pre-pubescent "angel voices."

Reference:(https://www.theguardian.com/music/2002/aug/05/classicalmusicandopera.artsfeatures)

898.

Divine Brown used the money stemming from her liaison with Hugh Grant to get her out of prostitution and get her kids into private school.

Reference: (https://en.wikipedia.org/wiki/Estella_Marie_Thompson)

899.

Dawn dish soap is made from petroleum which makes it better at cleaning oil and grease, especially from animals affected by oil spills.

Reference: (https://www.npr.org/templates/story/story.php?storyId=127999735)

900.

Researchers hypothesize that the European Bison originated as a result of a hybrid between two other species. They refer to this hypothetical ancestor as the "Higgs Bison".

Reference: (https://en.wikipedia.org/wiki/European_bison)

901.

New Zealand was uninhabited until 1250 to 1300 A.D.

Reference: (https://en.wikipedia.org/wiki/New_Zealand#History)

902.

There are only 20 to 25 true blimps in the world.

Reference: (http://www.vanwagneraerial.com/blog/history-of-the-metlife-blimp-and-van-wagner-airship-group)

903.

Canada has a program where volunteers will give rides to intoxicated people for free.

Reference: (https://operationrednose.com/history)

904.

Joysticks were eventually moved to the left of the buttons on arcade cabinets in an effort to make games more difficult to control.

Reference: (https://www.youtube.com/watch?v=LwyKx8TvRcE)

905.

Indian Spies confirmed Pakistan's nuclear program by analyzing the hair samples snatched from the floor of barber shops. However, the Indian Prime Minister accidentally informed the Pakistani President about their nuclear capabilities. Pakistan then eliminated Indian Spies who provided secret information.

Reference: (https://en.wikipedia.org/wiki/Research_and_Analysis_Wing)

906.

Jimmy Carter's chief of staff once allegedly commented, of the Egyptian ambassador's wife's breasts, "I have always wanted to see the pyramids."

Reference: (https://en.wikipedia.org/wiki/Hamilton_Jordan)

907.

Billions of Argentine ants belong to a single global mega-colony spanning Europe, Japan, and California.

Reference: (http://news.bbc.co.uk/earth/hi/earth_news/newsid_8127000/8127519.stm)

908.

Migingo Island, a tiny 2,000-square-metre island in Lake Victoria, has a population density of 65,500 people per square kilometer, or 169,600 people per square mile.

Reference: (https://en.wikipedia.org/wiki/Migingo_Island)

909.

Time Magazine published a list of the "Top 10 College Dropouts." Making the list: Bill Gates, Steve Jobs, Frank Lloyd Wright, Buckminster Fuller, James Cameron, Mark Zuckerberg, Tom Hanks, Harrison Ford, Lady Gaga, and Tiger Woods.

Reference:(http://content.time.com/time/specials/packages/completelist/0,29569,1988080,00.html)

910.

In 1700 India, present day India, Pakistan and Bangladesh, contributed 24.4% of world's economy with 25% of total industrial output.

Reference: (https://en.wikipedia.org/wiki/Economic_history_of_India)

911.

Dashrath Manjhi carved out a chunk of a mountain, with only simple tools, on his own, for 22 years to cut off 30 miles of travel after his wife's travel injury.

Reference: (https://ofdollarsanddata.com/great-things-take-time-7b509f4d5e03)

912.

Brooke Shields had featured in a Playboy publication called Sugar and Spice when aged only 10 years old in 1975.

Reference: (http://theconversation.com/playboy-brooke-shields-and-the-fetishisation-of-young-girls-85255)

913.

The 1700 Cascadia earthquake may have caused a legendary landslide that dammed the entire Columbia River Gorge, between Washington and Oregon. Natives called this 3.5 mile, 200 foot tall passageway the Bridge of the Gods.

Reference: (https://en.wikipedia.org/wiki/Bridge_of_the_Gods_(land_bridge))

914.

Hoover was only 29 when he became head of the FBI. Also, he fired and banned all female employees.

Reference: (https://en.wikipedia.org/wiki/J._Edgar_Hoover#Head_of_the_Radical_Division)

915.

Franklin D. Roosevelt is related, by blood or marriage, to a total of eleven presidents: Washington, John Adams, John Quincy Adams, Madison, Taylor, William Henry Harrison, Benjamin Harrison, Van Buren, Grant, and Taft.

Reference: (https://periodicpresidents.com/tag/presidents-related-to-each-other/)

916.

There have been more deaths than live births in Germany for every one of the last 45 years.

Reference: (https://en.wikipedia.org/wiki/Demographics_of_Germany#Statistics_since_1900)

917.

Central Park's Lamp Posts have a unique 4 digit code that will geolocate you anywhere in the park.

Reference: (https://youtu.be/mRx6UsHl0jU)

918.

Għana is a traditional Maltese folk music where two singers debate while playing instruments to the rhythm of their arguments.

Reference: (https://en.wikipedia.org/wiki/G%C4%A7ana_(folk_music)#Spirtu_Pront)

919.

A 106 year old fresh fruit cake was discovered in Antarctica that looked edible.

Reference: (http://www.sciencetimes.com/articles/17777/20170816/106-years-old-fresh-fruitcake-discovered-in-antarctica-that-looked-edible.htm)

920.

There have been 2 F3 tornadoes in California.

Reference: (http://www.tornadohistoryproject.com/tornado/California/F3/map)

921.

The Order of the Smile is an international award given by children to adults distinguished in their love, care and aid for children.

Reference: (https://en.wikipedia.org/wiki/Order_of_the_Smile)

922.

When fluoride was first introduced to American water supplies in the 1940s and 1950s, it was criticized as a Communist plot to socialize medicine and deplete the brain power of American children.

Reference: (https://hydrationanywhere.com/what-is-fluoride-doing-in-my-water/)

923.

Sign language is one of three official languages of New Zealand.

Reference: (http://archive.stats.govt.nz/Census/2013-census/profile-and-summary-reports/quickstats-culture-identity/languages.aspx)

924.

Irish American actor Robert De Niro was raised by an openly gay Catholic father and an atheist mother in New York just two generations after his family fled Ireland to escape the famine.

Reference: (https://www.irishpost.com/entertainment/7-things-never-knew-robert-de-niros-surprising-irish-roots-151703)

925.

Amanda America Dickson was regarded as one of the wealthiest Southern socialites of the 19th century. Dickson was taken from her 12 year old mother and raised on her wealthy planter father's estate. Inheriting it upon his death, the case was taken to the Supreme Court.

Reference: (https://www.georgiaencyclopedia.org/articles/history-archaeology/amanda-america-dickson-1849-1893)

926.

Puppies reach "peak cuteness" when they're between 6 and 8 weeks old.

Reference: (http://mentalfloss.com/article/545276/scientists-identify-when-puppies-reach-peak-cuteness)

927.

The record for the lowest final score in a high school basketball game is 2 - 0, a feat that has been "achieved" twice, both times in states without a shot clock.

Reference: (https://www.huffingtonpost.com/2015/02/03/high-school-basketball-low-score-2-0-alabama_n_6608360.html)

928.

The word laser originated as an acronym for "light amplification by stimulated emission of radiation."

Reference: (http://www.wiki-zero.net/index.php?q=aHR0cHM6Ly9lbi53aWtpcGVkaWEub3JnL3dpa2kvTGFzZXI)

929.

Chickens used to wear rose colored glasses to prevent them from cannibalizing one another.

Reference: (https://youtu.be/5xQD5G10W4U)

930.

Exercising and generally feeling happy releases something called brain-derived neurotrophic factor, which is involved in forming new neural pathways. Thus, exercise and happiness can help you in learning new things.

Reference: (http://www.sciencemag.org/news/2013/10/how-exercise-beefs-brain)

931.

Roland "the Farter" was hired to fart on cue at Christmas for 12th century English Monarchs.

Reference: (https://www.atlasobscura.com/articles/the-true-story-of-roland-the-farter-and-how-the-internet-killed-professional-flatulence)

932.

Africa is closer to Canada than the United States. Africa is closer to Maine than Florida.

Reference: (https://en.wikipedia.org/wiki/Quoddy_Head_State_Park)

933.

Annie Oakley first rose to fame at the age of 15 after beating a traveling sharpshooter, whom she later married.

Reference: (https://www.history.com/news/10-things-you-may-not-know-about-annie-oakley)

934.

Uber hasn't had an effect on drunken-driving deaths.

Reference: (https://www.npr.org/sections/thetwo-way/2016/07/29/487906925/uber-hasnt-had-an-effect-on-drunken-driving-deaths-study-finds)

935.

Cadaver dogs have been trained to find bodies in up to 49 feet of water.

Reference: (https://www.forensicmag.com/news/2015/09/cadaver-dogs-locate-underwater-corpses)

936.

The Wall in Game of Thrones was inspired by Hadrian's Wall.

Reference: (https://www.youtube.com/watch?v=bhpQwiz0Gq0)

937.

Bismarck rejected expansionism, saying of Wilhelm II: "That young man wants war with Russia, and would like to draw his sword straight away...". And upon his crowning: "Alas, my poor grandchildren." His grandson would end up in captured by Russians in World War II.

Reference: (https://www.cambridge.org/core/books/kaiser-wilhelm-ii/bismarcks-fall-from-power-18891890/6C72271128811D96FACB19BC1396B780)

938.

The two Matrix sequels were so reliant on digital effects that they used a total of 8 square kilometers of green screen.

Reference: (https://www.matrixfans.net/interview-with-david-thomson-blue-and-green-screen-coordinator-australia-from-the-matrix-reloaded-and-revolutions-2003/)

939.

Some hotel towels have RFID microchips sewn into them to know if you stole them.

Reference: (https://www.usatoday.com/story/travel/roadwarriorvoices/2015/02/06/yes-your-hotel-knows-that-you-just-stole-that-towel-because-they-sewed-a-microchip-in-it/83191436/)

940.

"Uncle Tom" was the hero in the novel, who refused to whip his fellow slaves and defended them with his life.

Reference:(https://en.wikipedia.org/w/index.php?title=Uncle_Tom%27s_Cabin&mobileaction=toggle_view_desktop)

941.

The Feigenson brothers, who developed Faygo, were originally bakers from Russia. The soda first became available in 1907 and came in three flavors: grape, strawberry, and fruit punch which were based on the brother's original cake frosting recipes.

Reference: (https://en.wikipedia.org/wiki/Faygo#History)

942.

A shamrock is a specific three-leaf variety of the clover family of plants, and only shamrocks, not four-leaf varieties of clovers, are the national symbol of Ireland.

Reference: (https://www.forrent.com/blog/food-entertaining/shamrock-and-a-four-leaf-clover/)

943.

In 1996, a Canadian man fled Canada and thought someone was out to kill him, took his money and drove to Knoxville, Tennessee. He ended up dead in a parking lot with his money around his half-naked body. Police reports show the man was killed by a blow to the stomach. The case remains unsolved.

Reference: (https://en.wikipedia.org/wiki/Murder_of_Blair_Adams)

944.

The kidnapping of Peggy Ann Bradnick resulted in a massive manhunt of over 1,000 federal, state, and local law officers and had one FBI agent killed.

Reference: (https://en.wikipedia.org/wiki/Kidnapping_of_Peggy_Ann_Bradnick#Kidnapping)

945.

The Red Sky at Morning rhyme is generally correct in the mid-latitude areas of the Earth.

Reference: (https://en.wikipedia.org/wiki/Red_sky_at_morning)

946.

Sacha Baron Cohen left the Freddie Mercury biopic over creative differences with Queen; he was told Mercury died in the middle of the film. Impressed, he thought they meant a non-linear story structure like "Pulp Fiction" but realized the second half would be how the band "carried on."

Reference: (https://www.rollingstone.com/movies/news/sacha-baron-cohen-explains-departure-from-freddie-mercury-biopic-20160308)

947.

Sea turtles can get a strain of the herpes virus from polluted coastal waters that can cause tumors and mortality.

Reference: (https://www.cabi.org/isc/datasheet/82638)

948.

The Bank of Canada ruled that production of banknotes in the Birds of Canada series would be revised to require 100% cotton fiber in 1984. Now, all banknotes in the series are considered unfit for circulation, as none of the banknotes contain the minimum security feature of a metallic stripe.

Reference: (https://en.wikipedia.org/wiki/Birds_of_Canada_(banknotes))

949.

Among players taken in the 1998 NFL draft, only Peyton Manning earned more in his professional sports career than his college backup quarterback, Todd Helton who out earned the rest of the draft class as a MLB player with a career tally of $141,000,000.

Reference: (http://www.spotrac.com/mlb/colorado-rockies/todd-helton-257/)

950.

Three young women from Korea were huge stars in the U.S. back in the 1960s, and were arguably the first K-Pop band.

Reference: (https://foto.gettyimages.com/archive/tributes/k-pop-in-the-usa-recalling-the-fabulous-kim-sisters/)

951.

Nelson Mandela had read "Things Fall Apart" when he was in prison on Robben Island and he described the author, Chinua Achebe: "The writer in whose company the prison walls fell down."

Reference: (https://blog.oup.com/2013/03/achebe/)

952.

Up until 1970, women of the Apatani tribe in India had to plug their nose as a rite of passage. It signified them becoming an adult and was believed to prevent men in other tribes from kidnapping them because of their beauty.

Reference: (http://www.odditycentral.com/pics/the-weird-nose-plugs-of-the-apatani-women.html)

953.

The square patch on the outside of your backpack is used to tie things to, such as shoes.

Reference: (https://www.youtube.com/watch?v=CNuRCY-TO28)

954.

There was a Hamas TV show for children which had its version of Mickey Mouse who was killed off by an Israeli.

Reference: (https://en.wikipedia.org/wiki/Tomorrow%27s_Pioneers)

955.

When bodybuilder Bill Pettis accidentally drowned in a creek bed in Pennsylvania 2016, he was found with a duffel bag which contained photos of him training in his heyday, including photos taken with his bodybuilding companions such as Arnold Schwarzenegger.

Reference: (https://www.greatestphysiques.com/bill-pettis/)

956.

There are turtle tunnels in Japan to save them from being run over by trains.

Reference: (https://www.boredpanda.com/turtle-tunnel-train-track-safety-japan-railways/)

957.

There is evidence that suggests Abraham Lincoln was not born in Kentucky, but was instead born in Bostic, North Carolina.

Reference: (http://www.bosticlincolncenter.com/background.htm)

958.

There were an extra 4 minutes in Michael Jackson's "Black or White" video that was censored by the networks.

Reference: (https://brobible.com/guyism/article/michael-jackson-black-or-white-uncovered/)

959.

There is a chocolate museum in Cologne that showcases the entire history of chocolate, from its beginnings with the Olmecs, Maya and Aztecs to contemporary products and production methods. A feature attraction is the 3-metre-high chocolate fountain for visitors to sample.

Reference: (https://en.wikipedia.org/wiki/Imhoff-Schokoladenmuseum)

960.

Dortmund University in Germany has its own 3 kilometer long suspended monorail system that runs through the campus.

Reference: (https://www.railway-technology.com/projects/h-bahn/)

961.

Rian Johnson wanted to show extreme violence in "The Last Jedi's" final battle, but couldn't do so in a PG-13 movie. To solve this, the planet Crait was covered in a layer of salt which, when displaced by the fighting, revealed a red landscape and made the battlefield appear drenched in blood.

Reference: (https://www.cinemablend.com/news/2302331/what-crait-symbolized-in-star-wars-the-last-jedi-according-to-rian-johnson)

962.

Saguenay–Lac-Saint-Jean is considered the heartland of the Quebec sovereignty movement and a popular vacation destination in the summer for residents of the more urban regions of the province.

Reference: (https://en.wikipedia.org/wiki/Saguenay%E2%80%93Lac-Saint-Jean)

963.

Since 2015, the soundwave of "O Canada" sung by fans at a bar has been stitched on to every Canadian National Soccer Jersey.

Reference: (https://www.winnipegfreepress.com/wfpfeatured/canadas-new-soccer-kit-features-sound-wave-graphic-of-o-canada-138666494.html)

964.

Another name for an icosahedron is a gyroelongated pentagonal bipyramid.

Reference: (https://www.youtube.com/watch?v=FqCZhSIXcv4&feature=youtu.be&t=10m33s)

965.

An early version of the remote control looked like a gun.

Reference: (https://gizmodo.com/5912687/the-first-wireless-tv-remote-looked-and-worked-like-a-sci-fi-ray-gun)

966.

Harrison Ford had a brief stint as a cameraman. He was offered to fill the role of second camera or grip for a documentary about The Doors, called "Feast of Friends," after director Paul Ferrara had hired him for carpentry work on his house.

Reference: (https://www.stuff.co.nz/entertainment/film/74650308/Harrison-Ford-once-shot-The-Doors-Jim-Morrison)

967.

Ants can't climb surfaces that have a talcum powder rubbing alcohol mix or petroleum jelly.

Reference: (http://www.antscanada.com/ant-care/)

968.

A Japanese exchange student wearing a white tuxedo was shot and killed by a property owner after showing up by mistake at a wrong house for a Halloween party. His last words were, "We're here for the party!". The court ruled the killer not guilty.

Reference: (https://en.wikipedia.org/wiki/Death_of_Yoshihiro_Hattori)

969.

The New York Supreme Court officially ruled that a house was haunted when a buyer was allowed to back out of a deal from the owner because she didn't disclose that the house was haunted.

Reference: (http://nyacknewsandviews.com/2014/10/nsl_legally_haunted_house/)

970.

The valve on most roasted coffee bags is a one way valve to let out CO_2 released by the beans as well as keep out oxygen and humidity that would degrade the shelf life.

Reference: (https://en.wikipedia.org/wiki/Coffee_roasting#Packaging)

971.

On August 25th, 1835, the New York Sun published a 6 article hoax about the discovery of life on the Moon, calling the inhabitants Moonbat's with a population of 4,200,000,000. The discoveries were falsely attributed to Sir John Herschel, one of the best-known contemporary astronomers of that time.

Reference: (https://en.wikipedia.org/wiki/Great_Moon_Hoax)

972.

About half of Americans make their "s" sounds with their tongue tip down, and about half with their tongue tip up.

Reference: (https://youtu.be/lZSCGZphjq0?t=4m30s)

973.

RCA spent 17 years trying to find a way to put movies on vinyl records. In 1981, they finally achieved this, marketing the SelectaVision system. Unfortunately, by the time they finished researching the system, someone had invented the VHS video tape.

Reference: (https://www.atlasobscura.com/articles/the-doomed-effort-to-make-videos-go-vinyl)

974.

For 1988's Midnight Run, production executives suggested replacing Charles Grodin with Cher to provide "sexual overtones."

Reference: (https://en.wikipedia.org/wiki/Midnight_Run#Production)

975.

We lose the ability to understand grammar if we didn't learn our first language till the age of 13.

Reference: (https://www.youtube.com/watch?v=DwyWMbjstnY&feature=youtu.be)

976.

NASA has their own SWAT team.

Reference: (https://kscpartnerships.ksc.nasa.gov/Partnering-Opportunities/Capabilities-and-Testing/Support-Services/Security)

977.

Arrichion, an Ancient Greek wrestler, was declared the champion of the 54th Olympics wrestling event, despite having died.

Reference: (http://ejmas.com/jcs/jcsart_hollenback_0903.htm)

978.

King Tut had a cleft lip, a clubfoot, suffered from malaria, and was a, "proud product of the practice of royal sister–brother incest."

Reference: (https://www.thegreatcoursesdaily.com/the-mask-of-tutankhamun/)

979.

The Trans Canada Trail is the longest recreational, multi-use trail network in the world spanning 24 thousand kilometers.

Reference: (https://thegreattrail.ca/)

980.

The Aborigines of Australia were the first people to set foot on the continent, somewhere between 40,000 and 60,000 years ago.

Reference: (https://people.howstuffworks.com/aborigine.htm)

981.

An unconscious prisoner was declared dead by three doctors before he was discovered to be alive when he started snoring on the autopsy table.

Reference: (https://www.independent.co.uk/news/world/europe/prison-inmate-dead-wake-up-mortuary-spain-three-doctors-pronounced-gonzalo-montoya-jimenez-oviedo-a8149066.html)

982.

Owning a dog was banned in China throughout the 1980's, and 1990's. The rule was lifted in 2003.

Reference: (https://www.pri.org/stories/2014-08-13/china-denounces-pet-dogs-filthy-imports-west)

983.

The average age of a World War II veteran is 100.

Reference: (https://www.usatoday.com/story/news/nation-now/2014/11/11/surviving-world-war-two-veterans/18805003/)

984.

On September 8th, 2009, Sgt. Dakota Meyer disobeyed a direct order to pull back from his position so he could rescue wounded soldiers from a firefight a mile away. He ended up going back five times, saving the lives of 36 soldiers, saying "That's what you do for a brother".

Reference: (http://www.salem-news.com/articles/december052011/dakota-meyer-tk.php)

985.

The Gong Show had one episode where every act sung the song "Feelings."

Reference: (https://www.youtube.com/watch?v=F9U0e_dXSUQ)

986.

Sprint Football is a form of American Football in which the participants must be 178 pounds or less and 5% or less body fat. It is a varsity sport at some universities and many famous people, including President Jimmy Carter, have played it.

Reference: (https://www.sprintfootball.com/rules)

987.

The Queen Mother always carries a handbag in public and can use it to discretely send unspoken instructions to her staff such as her desire to end a conversation with someone or her rediness to depart a location.

Reference: (https://www.urbo.com/content/heres-why-the-queen-always-carries-her-purse/)

988.

The Great Picture is a gigantic 111 by 32 foot photograph taken by converting a hangar into a massive camera using 21 gallons of photosensitive Silver Halide. It took 80 people five hours to develop after being taken.

Reference: (https://en.wikipedia.org/wiki/The_Great_Picture)

989.

The Spider-Man tray scene wasn't CGI and took Tobey Maguire 156 takes.

Reference: (https://www.independent.co.uk/arts-entertainment/films/news/that-spider-man-tray-scene-wasn-t-cgi-took-tobey-maguire-156-takes-a7358816.html)

990.

"Brilliant Chang" was England's notorious 20th century drug dealer. Originally from China, Chang scandalized English society in the trial that followed the untimely death of one of his female clients. Portrayed by the press as the embodiment of the "Yellow Peril", he was eventually deported.

Reference: (https://en.wikipedia.org/wiki/Brilliant_Chang)

991.

Lay's Potato Chips are known as Walkers in the U.K.

Reference: (https://en.wikipedia.org/wiki/Walkers_(snack_foods))

992.

"Bohemian Rhapsody" has its origins in 1968 when Freddie Mercury was in college. The "Mama, just killed a man" section started off as a stand-alone piece which Freddie called "The Cowboy Song" because he thought that it had an Old West feeling to it.

Reference: (http://mentalfloss.com/article/70634/10-operatic-facts-about-bohemian-rhapsody)

993.

Portland, Oregon's name was decided by a coin flip after Portland, Maine. There was a 50% chance that the city would be called Boston.

Reference: (http://www.naosmm.org/confer/port-or/history.html)

994.

The Fetterman Fight was a massacre of 81 U.S. Army troops by plains Indians, 10 years before General Custer's last stand.

Reference: (https://en.wikipedia.org/wiki/Fetterman_Fight)

995.

Rooster State Park is a state park in Oregon. The park's name comes from Rooster Rock, a large phallus shaped basalt formation. It was named Iwash, or penis, by the Native Americans and Cock Rock by Lewis and Clark. The name was changed to Rooster Rock to avoid offending the public.

Reference: (https://en.wikipedia.org/wiki/Rooster_Rock_State_Park)

996.

California produces 82% of the world's almonds.

Reference: (http://www.latimes.com/business/la-fi-california-almonds-20140112-story.html)

997.

The acceptance rate of Harvard (5.6%) is twice that of Walmart jobs (2.6%).

Reference: (http://www.businessinsider.com/things-more-selective-than-harvard-2017-4)

998.

Hungary welcomes more tourists each year than its total population.

Reference: (https://en.wikipedia.org/wiki/Hungary)

999.

When Monique Macias' father, the President of Equatorial Guinea, foresaw his own execution, personal arrangements were made with Kim Il-sung to take Monique and her siblings to live in North Korea. She remained there for 15 years and later wrote a memoir.

Reference: (https://www.independent.co.uk/news/world/asia/extraordinary-images-reveal-life-in-north-korea-for-african-dictators-daughter-exiled-there-for-15-8855913.html)

1000.

Geckos can't climb Teflon.

Reference: (https://www.youtube.com/watch?v=wLpQ5EzF-q8&feature=share)

Made in the USA
Columbia, SC
08 October 2021